PRAISE FOR *LESSONS FROM ZACHARY*

"There is no better story to role-model how a coaching mindset can transform difficult life situations into a radically fulfilling life."

— MARSHALL GOLDSMITH, recognized in November as the World's #1 Leadership Thinker at the *Thinkers 50* ceremony in London. Author of *Triggers*, a #1 *New York Times* and *Wall Street Journal* bestseller and one of the *Amazon.com* Editor's Choice Business Books of the Year

"Sandy's story reminds us that contrary to what most of us believe, happiness does not simply happen to us. It's something that we make happen, and it results from our doing our best."

— MIHALY CSIKSZENTMIHALYI, worlds' leading researcher on positive psychology. Author of *Flow: The Psychology of Optimal Experience* and 120 other books, articles or book chapters. Distinguished Professor of Psychology and Management of Claremont Graduate University

"*Lessons from Zachary* illustrates what can become available when we engage in a new kind of conversation, discovering and unleashing the human possibility in us all."

— JOSEPH JAWORSKI, best-selling author of *Synchronicity: The Inner Path of Leadership* and co-founder, Chairman of Generon International

"Sandy Scott has experienced many challenges. Instead of becoming hardened and angry, she has learned from the challenges… and she has thrived. *Lessons from Zachary* doesn't just tell a story, it sends a powerful message of hope, possibility and encouragement as we walk through our own unexpected challenges."

— LINDA MILLER, Global Liaison of Coaching Ken Blanchard Companies. Author of *Coaching in Organizations: Best Coaching Practices from the Ken Blanchard Companies*

"I highly recommend this book to anyone experiencing a transition in life. Sandy imparts deep personal stories and essential lessons necessary to live a meaningful life."

— DEB DAHL, Vice President Patient Care Innovation, Banner Health

"Sandy Scott shares her powerful story based on the solid research in the coaching industry and teaches us how to navigate difficult situations to live meaningful lives."

— LEANN THIEMAN, author *Chicken Soup for the Soul, Inspiration for Nurses*

Lessons *from* Zachary

TURNING DISABILITY INTO POSSIBILITY

SANDY SCOTT

INTERNATIONAL
PUBLISHING WORKS

Lessons from Zachary

For information about this title or to order other books and/or electronic media, contact the publisher:
International Publishing Works
P O Box 415
Bellvue, CO 80512-0415

ISBNs: 978-0-9975962-0-5 (print)
        978-0-9975962-1-2 (eBook)

Printed in the United States of America
Cover and Interior design: 1106 Design

TABLE OF CONTENTS

FOREWORD

I recall the first time I met Zachary and his parents. It was morning, and light shone through my eastern-facing window at Denver Children's Hospital and onto Zach's upturned face. This was 23 years ago. I recall that day and this child because, despite knowing the devastating diagnosis his parents had recently received, there before me was his smile, his amazing, responsive, interactive, smile. It was, and is, infectious.

As a physician board certified in both pediatrics and child neurology, I had finished training 16 years before Zach's visit and had recently accepted a faculty position in Colorado. The focus of my prior medical school and post graduate training was to be able to assess, diagnose, and treat as well as advise treatment of the broad areas of illness that might face me, attempting to fix problems. My formal training in those days was to prescribe and expect compliance from others. We were expected to focus on procedures, test, and the problems, and be the expert. After my adult and child-neurology training, I felt something was missing in my training and took on a child psychiatry fellowship, studying family systems and learning theory as they apply to children's' behavioral issues.

At the time I first met Sandy and Jonathan, I was aware of the grief process they had entered. But after reading Sandy's book now, 24 years later, I am reminded of how my own heart and manner of practice was shaped by their story and on how physicians can influence the paths of grieving. I am increasingly aware how physicians in today's complex and often demoralizing healthcare environment can impact the patient experience in ways both new and yet reminiscent of why most of us became doctors.

Today medical training includes experiential learning in ethics, quality improvement and leadership skills, calling for young physicians to be team members sharing the responsibility of patient-centered care. In fact, all providers—physicians, nurses, therapists, pharmacologists, educators, and social workers—are in the vanguard of a new frontier in medicine. In cases like Zach's, those of us paid to be caregivers in the lives of those disabled can alter the trajectory of their families' lives and their own. Faced with a terrible diagnosis, devastating to the receiver and, often, bearer of the bad news, individuals may eventually stagnate emotionally or recover. But some actually thrive. This book is about those trajectories and how collaboration and coaching can lead to a more fulfilling life for self and others.

Rather than cutting ourselves off from our inner motivations and drives, slaves to the electronic medical record and submitting to the unlimited opportunity to work longer hours, Sandy invites us to align our personal aspirations with our personal and professional ambitions. We are encouraged to grow our own self-awareness so that we might serve others more authentically and wholeheartedly, literally altering the trajectory of how we see others as well as ourselves and the quality of our lives. We can learn about our emotional IQ (the EQ), coaching skills and "mindfulness," all of which dramatically impact the way we deliver care to others and support one another to live meaningful lives. We who are blessed to be inserted into the lives of those seeking medical help may live the day when we embrace a new journey of discovery, wholeness, and courage, and lead others more wisely.

Sandy's remarkable story leads the reader on an amazing journey, chock full of unforeseen twists and turns. We live life with her, searching, finding, exploring, and, through an amazing series of decisions, setbacks and triumphs, to eventually achieve peace, for herself and her sons, and success in both personal and corporate arenas. I was Director of Quality at a large urban pediatric hospital here in Colorado and have walked some of the paths tread by Sandy in her search for meaning in the corporate healthcare setting. Her story will resonate strongly with parents with or without kids with disabilities, teachers, physicians, healthcare leaders, corporate coaches, and CEOs everywhere.

This is a book that speaks to our hearts and minds. I couldn't put it down.

— Thomas T. Reiley, MD
Golden, Colorado
February 2016

INTRODUCTION

"Suppose tonight while you sleep, a miracle happens.
When you awake tomorrow morning, what will you see
yourself doing, thinking, or believing about yourself that
will tell you a miracle has happened in your life?"

— Dr. Steve DeShazer and Insoo Kim Berg

The idea for this book came to me in the midst of a tantrum. During an early morning walk, I was becoming increasingly frustrated that, though my life seemed to be stable, I was feeling restless. I wanted to take a risk and expose my inner awareness of something, even though I still couldn't name it. I wanted to reconnect with some kind of creativity and discipline that was swirling inside of me, and perhaps in some crazy way, help others move through difficult experiences to live meaningful lives.

So, on November 14th, 2014, my partner, Mike, and I went to a local Italian restaurant. I requested that we not drink, because I wanted to get real in a way that I hadn't been before. I told Mike that my vision was to write 1,000 words every morning before work. I wanted to simply show up to the page, light a candle, open my heart and just put the words down. I mentioned this could be highly disruptive to our relationship, in part because it would take a lot of time to follow this new path. Actually, the part I was most scared of was writing things that could be upsetting to people, including Mike. He listened and then told me that it turned him on when I was being so fully myself.

I started the next morning. I wrote about getting married, giving birth, getting divorced, and fighting the human experience the whole way. Over time, I felt a softness about topics I had cut off from—as well as a new fierceness to give voice to things I had never told myself or said aloud to anyone else.

Historically, a person who talked about "disabilities" and "possibilities" was considered to be a person in denial—out of touch with reality. I had not paid attention to this until my first son's birth, though on hearing of Zachary's diagnosis as severely physically and intellectually disabled, I became keenly aware that people with disabilities were often segregated, separated from the possibility of living a meaningful life. I had not grown up with knowing anyone with a disability, and I quickly learned part of the reason. Up until 1990, if a child was born with significant disabilities, there were resources to support him or her, though it often meant leaving home to live in an institution-like setting. It was normal for a child with severe disabilities to be separated from their local community and family. If the child stayed with his or her family, there wasn't much support to guide the family toward new hopes and dreams, so they often shifted into a mode of simply surviving, not thriving.

Children and teens with disabilities and their families were held hostage to the beliefs and assumptions of people who surrounded them. If people didn't connect with a child with disabilities, then the family lived a life of fighting to belong somewhere, even if it was a place of loneliness. Yet in 1990, the year before Zachary was born, a new public policy was passed. The IDEA (Individuals with Disabilities Education Act) was a federal law designed to protect the rights of children with disabilities by ensuring everyone received a free, appropriate education regardless of ability. This meant children with disabilities and their families did not need to be sentenced to a separate life. The new public policy would invoke a whole new conversation! It would invite families and the people associated with ordinary places children and families spend time to come together in new ways. The professionals who were early adopters of this new paradigm would be responsible for inviting a new way of being for agency providers, educators, clergy, recreation instructors, healthcare leaders, and the people of ordinary communities.

Before giving birth to Zachary, I, like many other people, had no understanding of what life was like for a person with a disability. I didn't want to know about the world of disabilities, and I didn't want to know how it impacted families. But when the doctor informed me my 11-day-old baby would maybe live a year, a door opened into a new world of, yes, heartbreak, but also possibilities.

As a new mom, raising Zachary and then Taylor, I started my own journey of despair, hope, and, finally, joy and gratitude. In the quiet spaces of not knowing how to raise a nonverbal son with significant medical complexities, feeling shamed at being a single mom, and not having a predictable, traditional job, I began to let go of the way my life was *supposed* to be and carve out moments to show up to the life that was now mine.

Unfortunately, there are still too many people with disabilities living a life based in disconnectedness, isolation, and minimal sense of belonging. In fact, this is true for many of us—disabled or not. Each of us will inevitably encounter life experiences that knock us off our imagined life plan. The difference is that many of us can still access hundreds of invisible supports as we navigate our own difficult life experiences. We can mask, move through, or numb ourselves to our life struggles. But when people with disabilities hit a bump in the road or have a bad day, they also have the compounded work of accessing everyday natural supports, and they are often dependent upon someone else's mood. They must navigate added hurdles because many people have a habit of seeing people with disabilities as broken.

Being a mom to Zachary and Taylor opened my eyes to our human capacity for strength and compassion—for others as well as for ourselves. Disabled or not, we all need purpose, hope, and love. We also need the courage to cultivate our own awareness of how we filter the world. Raising my boys gave me a direct experience of seeing the world through "beginners eyes." I was forced to live one moment at a time, and in doing so, I discovered the power of curiosity. I had learned in my coach training what was needed in the moment. One day at a time, I became aware of this new way of thinking and participating in our life as it began to unfold. In doing so, I bumped into other people more experienced than me, and together we stumbled into moments of flow and creating new realities together.

It excites me to imagine how more of us might be able to invoke new and creative ways of influencing the future of families, agencies, and administrations who have relationships with people who have disabilities. For me, this journey has been deeply meaningful, and I owe tremendous thanks for the people who have walked beside us as we aligned ourselves with the new "generative" thinking. These moments of curiosity have opened up new spaces to live, work, and recreate in the outdoors together. It can be difficult for us to tap our full potential when we try to figure it out by ourselves, if we are marginalized and separated from community. We can, however, build relationships so that we can shape and impact one another. As we live and work in proximity to each other, we can experience mini-breakthroughs of what comes naturally and what gives us energy. These moments can be strung together like pearls, bringing us a sense of deep fulfillment and inner beauty.

In writing this book, the more I took the risk to tell myself the truth about my own life experience, the more I could feel myself becoming who I really am. Inevitably, I noticed more about my own values and my own story. As I walked in the dark each morning, I felt less alone in the mess of my own humanity, less fragmented.

Lessons from Zachary is about the paradox of fulfillment. It is a story of what is possible when one part of our world is a struggle while another part brings a whisper of being present and fulfilled. It is written for people who are curious about how to leverage their own strengths and talents to navigate their difficult experiences and live meaningful lives. After 25 years of coaching/training and the experience of raising Zachary and Taylor, I have yearned to pass my hard-won wisdom on to others.

What the world needs is for each of us to play to our strengths, live more authentically, and work more wholeheartedly. Together may we co-create moments to be present with one another beyond our labels, beyond words, to create the future as it emerges. May you discover more of your life lessons as I share mine.

Love, love, love,

PREFACE

As I finalize this book, something has been weighing heavy on my mind: how to tell the truth to the best of my recollection without hurting anyone.

What I've learned throughout this process is that it is OK to share my own experiences and insights. I'm still learning how to do this, and so throughout this book I have worked to be transparent in what I have learned, what I have felt, and the insights I've gathered along the way. To protect other people, I have changed some names, though the situations are all true.

It is my hope that by sharing my full story, I can champion others to live more fully into their true story.

PART I

The journey begins into unexpected territory...

DIAGNOSIS

I n August 1991 I was feeling very pregnant, and exhausted waiting for Hannah/Chloe or Zachary/Hunter/Mason to be born. I had done about as much preparation as any new mom could. I was ready to wear a normal sized ankle-length white lace nightgown, nursing, snuggling, sleeping, and walking together in our new hoped-for-dreamed-of family. I had rehearsed our new life over and over in my mind. We were ready.

Zachary was born August 30th. His Apgar scores were 8 and then 9. 10 was the highest, so I knew all was well. We had a typical delivery, went home. I felt so liberated! I was released from the grind of my job, all the preparations were in place, and I finally got to meet our baby, Zachary. His name came from the John Denver song "Zachary and Jennifer." My eyes used to get all misty in college when I listened to the lyrics:

> Oh, we want to call him Zachary
> We'll raise him in the mountains
> He'll bathe in crystal fountains
> Shining laughter in the sun

Oh, we want to live forever
In this mirror sea tomorrow
All the joy and all the sorrow
We can only hope to share

Zachary slept in our bed the first few nights. I didn't want to sleep separately from him; I wanted his heartbeat to be near my heartbeat. I nursed him, and Jonathan helped change diapers. Zachary didn't cry. He was so much easier to take care of than other newborns I had heard stories about.

When Zachary was a few days old, I took him to the office at Kinko's where I used to work, though we only stayed a short time. One woman was talking about another new mom whose baby was diagnosed with something…. I didn't even stick around to hear about it. I felt terrible about the thoughts in my head, really nasty thoughts, like "I'm glad that's not my baby." I recall thinking if I were in that situation, it would be best for the baby to die. I couldn't imagine living a death sentence like that from the very beginning of life.

I had met my husband, Jonathan Turner, my senior year at the University of Iowa through a sign-up board. He had posted a note looking for passengers wanting to go from Iowa City to Maquoketa, Iowa, on the weekends. I did not have a car and wanted to visit my grandmother, so I called the number and joined a few others in the van as we carpooled north.

I began to visit my grandmother more often, in part because I liked Jonathan, though it wasn't love at first sight. It was as if I were part of a silent, Midwestern, arranged-marriage process, the rules of which were organized and sequential. The key elements were something like this:

- Mutual comfort with each other's age, Midwestern background, height, education, career path, and income potential.

- Our families both had roots in Maquoketa and seemed socio-economically compatible.

- Our families approved of each other (my grandparents and his parents lived in the same town).

- Jonathan and I talked and got to know each other well enough to feel comfortable.

It felt safe in his old blue Ford van. We are both tall—Jonathan is 6'2" while I'm 6'. We were both born in Iowa. I was raised in the Methodist church; Jonathan was raised Lutheran. Neither of us had ever experimented with a single drug or drank alcohol. But beyond that, we were opposites. I drank orange juice in the afternoon drives to Maquoketa, and Jonathan wondered why I didn't drink it in the morning. I always carried a small bag of baby carrots with me and grazed on veggies and pretzels. Jonathan ate three meals a day, and when he was on the farm, dinner was the mid-day meal. I liked to talk about what I was learning in my classes—physics, ballet, life drawing of nudes, and real-life marketing issues. Jonathan was very private and didn't talk much. When he did, the subjects were Star Trek, software, hardware, and life on the farm where he grew up. We spoke different languages.

We didn't begin to date until after had I graduated and moved to Colorado. I had a bachelor's degree in business and struggled to find a job. My roommate spent the summer de-tasseling corn, and I accepted a job recruiting campers to attend a summer camp in Nederland, CO. When Jonathan visited, we camped in the Arapahoe National Forest on the edges of Rocky Mountain National Park. It was Jonathan's first time west of Iowa. I wasn't too nervous about trying to find my way in the next chapter of my life; I *was* nervous being alone with a guy in the woods. One morning, I got out of the tent to listen to the rushing water of the river beside us. I climbed on top of a giant, icy log to walk across, with both hands in my pockets. Near the end of this slippery wooden tightrope, I wiped out and landed in a pile of frozen pine needles. It was a metaphor for much of my relationship with Jonathan: a bit lonely finding my way, exploring, and failing.

My job in the mountains was tentative at best, so eventually I moved in with Jonathan in Iowa City, where he had a good job as an electrical engineer. His office building was 500 yards from the Kinko's Copies store I managed. It was my first real, grown-up job. We didn't develop friends or engage in many social activities. I told myself it was normal. We were earning paychecks instead of paying tuition, so this was a step in the right direction.

After three years of living in Iowa City, we moved to Fort Collins. Jonathan accepted a position with a computer hardware, software, and electronics company, and I became the new manager for the Kinko's near the campus of Colorado State University. We shared a car. Jonathan drove to work since his commute was farther. I walked to work each day and back home each night.

We became established in our new jobs and then in August of 1986 took a week off to fly back to Des Moines to get married. The ceremony was held inside the Botanical Garden, where we were immersed with our guests among exotic orchids, flowering plants, and a canopy of trees and palms. We said our vows and lit the candles as the misting system cooled the giant conservatory. We had a simple reception, more like a nice indoor picnic in the adjoining conference room. I felt like my life was going according to plan, though I continued to feel lonely. I couldn't understand why.

Jonathan and I were different in many ways. I tended to have a million great ideas that were rarely executed and noticed that in some conversations I would "lose" people. In our marriage, I often felt like a failure at communicating the most basic thoughts and feelings. Jonathan was very focused on the details, and I felt like we just couldn't find a common language. The strange part was that when we tended to our separate ways of being, living in parallel, things seemed to go well. We didn't argue. We didn't engage much beyond the business of living together. I didn't know what I didn't know, so this felt like a reasonable way to be in a marriage.

Eventually, we made the decision to buy a home in Fort Collins among a small group of houses that dotted county Road 15. A long strip of Russian olive trees bordered our two acres. The view to the west was wide-open pastures with expansive views of the Rocky Mountains. Inside, our home was a contemporary layout of separate rooms joined by a two-story atrium planter in the middle of the house. It was filled with natural light, and we dedicated one room to a baby grand piano, which Jonathan and I both played. I was filled with a sense of both loneliness and hope as we started the next chapter of our life: beginning a family.

By December 1990 I was pregnant and thrilled. I come from a Midwestern family, where the men work and the women stay home. Jonathan and I agreed I would leave my job to be a stay-at-home mom. This felt natural. In fact, I didn't know many women with careers. I was ready to leave Kinko's. I would stop traveling between Wyoming, Montana, and Colorado, where I managed the operations and finances of seven stores and get centered in our life in Fort Collins. Jonathan had a big garden in the backyard and a giant workshop in the three-car garage filled with a table saw, mitre saw, and myriad tools. It seemed we had all the essentials for a family.

After the birth, Jonathan rotated between setting up his new business downstairs in the basement and spending time with Zachary—he had left his job as a software engineer to start his own software company, the JMT Company (Jonathan Mark Turner). I nursed Zachary, walked around the neighborhood with him in our little front backpack, and began to settle into our quiet and easy new routines. Even the task of filling in Zachary's name on our homemade baby announcements I had individually water colored was easy. I added some extra doodles when Zachary napped in his homemade cradle and then stamped and mailed them to announce our perfect baby boy, who barely even cried.

Eleven days later on Sept. 10th, Zachary started crying, and I couldn't figure how to comfort him. We went to the clinic and agreed with the pediatrician that Zachary might have gotten gas in his belly from nursing. I had made a stir-fry for dinner the night before. Our female doctor had children of her own, and she gently recommended two things: give him pedialite and cut back on eating fresh crunchy vegetables.

That night, I was making dinner. Zachary was in the carrier against my chest and kept arching his back. He started screaming, so I offered him the pedialite. We rocked, walked, sat—nothing soothed him. My mom was visiting from New Jersey, and I could tell she was nervous. I called the clinic again, though I felt embarrassed, like some high-maintenance mom who couldn't manage a little crying. They said it was after hours and we would need to meet the doctor on call at the hospital. It felt a little extreme, but it was the only option.

I figured it was no big deal, so I left everything as it was in the kitchen. I could finish making dinner when we got home. I left the pasta on the counter and put a lid on the sauce. Jonathan and I headed to town for what we assumed would be a quick conversation with the doctor on call.

The next 24–48 hours are a blur. I remember phrases like:

"Ear infection."

"Infection."

"Meningitis."

"Encephalitis."

"Aseptic Infection."

"This is an emergency—get the blah, blah, blah staff in here immediately!"

I couldn't make sense of what was happening. We were surrounded by other people in the Emergency Room with head injuries, blood-soaked clothing, and weeping families. The nurse told me they were going to do a spinal tap on Zachary. I did not know what a spinal tap was.[1] They took him down a long, sterile, white hallway, and suddenly I could hear him scream from where Jonathan and I were in the ER waiting room. I didn't feel any connection to anyone except my baby. In that moment, I made a vow to never ever be separated from him again in a hospital. I felt paralyzed, blocked from my son by a wall of concrete and cut off from any feelings of connectedness to my husband by the invisible wall in our relationship. I felt helpless and hopeless standing outside the sterilized room surrounded by the smell of body odor, urine, and Lysol.

Before I knew it, Zachary was being admitted to the 3rd floor for pediatric patients. I wanted to take him home and start the day over again. It felt like everything was going off track, and I just wanted to get back to what I knew. We followed Zachary's little gurney up the elevator into his room. As we entered the empty patient room, I heard the new male doctor yell at the team of nurses because the critical staffs were not in the room, and he expected them to be there. It was evening, and the on-call staffs were being contacted. The mood of the room was intense. People were moving quickly, though not much was being said. Zachary's little room was not like his new baby room at home. Here were screens on the walls,

---

[1] Now I know what a spinal tap is. It is the careful insertion of a needle between the vertebrae of the lower back, avoiding the spinal cord but entering the spinal fluid space and allowing fluid to be collected for examination. A normal result rules out meningitis and encephalitis.

beeping sounds, computers on rollers, hoses connected to machines, metal cabinets with metal drawers. It felt like we were inside a giant computer. People were in uniforms adjusting radio-like dials and IV units.

On Sept. 12th, I was sitting in the family conference room of the 3rd floor when the doctor gave the diagnosis: severe cerebral palsy[2] and possible death by Zachary's first birthday. Despite having appeared normal to us at birth, Zachary had instead been born with hidden, severe brain damage, not uncommon, we later learned from talking with our doctors and other parents of kids born at term of normal pregnancies, labor, and delivery but who nevertheless develop cerebral palsy. Yes, a full 75% of kids like Zachary develop CP unexpectedly due to brain injury predating labor and with time enough to "recover" from the stress of the injury while still in the womb and thus appear mostly normal at birth. He had suddenly lost his ability to suck and swallow at day 11, and we have had no explanation, ever. Zachary had profound brain damage and would not be able to suck. We needed to learn how to gavage-feed him with a tube and talk about end-of-life issues. I suddenly felt I was in the middle of a Hallmark movie. As a young girl, I remember watching these movies on Sunday nights. The

---

[2]   Cerebral Palsy (CP) describes the condition of having brain ("cerebral") injury early in life severe enough to cause weakness, stiffness, incoordination, paralysis, or difficulty planning movement ("palsy"). 40% of kids with CP also have some degree of cognitive impairment, and 40–50% may also have seizures/epilepsy during their lives. The term, however, doesn't imply the cause of the brain damage. The causes of all neurologic conditions can be lumped into several broad categories: CITTIMIDDIPO: Congenital (malformations: blood-clotting disorders), Infection (meningitis, encephalitis, AIDS, etc, viral or bacterial), Trauma (crush injury as in a maternal/ fetal auto accident or profound misplacement of forceps during delivery), Tumor (congenital brain tumor), Ingestions (maternal alcohol consumption of a quart a day of hard alcohol during pregnancy; rarely cocaine) Metabolic (so-called inborn errors of metabolism, very rare, worsens with age; not usually a cause of CP), Inherited (blood-clotting disorders, genetic conditions arising as new mutations or passed on), Deprivational (being relatively deprived of essential vitamins; not usually considered causal of CP), Degenerative (any of the many neurologic diseases that are progressive; never the cause of the brain damage of CP, which by its nature, does not worsen), Idiopathic (an unfortunate cause implying that science has no explanation; Psychogenic (psychosomatic illness; never a cause of CP) and Organs (failures of other organs such as the heart, kidneys, or liver that may impact brain health; not causes of CP).

romance and tragedy of each film depended on people dealing with intense emotional themes. The people always defied the odds, though usually in the final five minutes of the show. All I needed was to stay engaged in this intense and temporary struggle so that we could get back to our life. I told myself, "If he lives to his first birthday, I will make a life-sized cake, give sparklers to everyone, and make Zachary his own personal flag."

Being in a hospital was unchartered, territory for me. I did not have experience with grief or navigating complex medical systems. I did not know what to do so I just started doing whatever I thought we would be doing if we didn't have a monster diagnosis to deal with. I held Zachary. I asked for a CD player and cranked really good music. Without any orientation of how to be Zachary's mom, I looked for clues about what other people thought I should be doing. Sometimes I just went along with the situation so people would think I was a good sport and a good mother.

As the mom of a very sick newborn, I was surrounded by a rotation of physicians, registered nurses, phlebotomists, epidemiologists, certified nurse assistants, nurse practitioners, pharmacists, physical therapists, nutritionists, social workers, clinical laboratory technicians, dieticians, diagnostic medical technicians, respiratory therapists, and more physicians. People in masks rotated day and night until night was day and I lost all sense of who I was. I had just left a world of managing copy stores to launch my new role in the world of motherhood. Suddenly, my identity was turned upside down, inside out, and then smashed to pieces.

Since entering the hospital, Zachary had been connected to tubes for oxygen and food. He was not able to suck or swallow, and the diagnosis at the time suggested that his brain may never allow him to breathe or swallow independently again. The doctors told us we would need to learn how to gavage-feed him.

The gavage training happened in the same family conference room at the end of the 3rd floor where we learned of Zachary's diagnosis the day before. We had some extended family standing around as we learned to insert a tube down Zachary's tiny throat and into his belly. Stethoscopes around our necks, we listened for specific sounds so that we didn't accidentally pour fluid into his lungs. I told myself this was just a mock trial and life would resume its more ordinary routines after we left the hospital.

On September 16th at 11:15AM, as we were gavage-feeding him, Zachary did his first independent suck and swallow. I ran to the nurse's station at the other end of the hallway to spread the news. There weren't any doctors around to tell. A few moments later, he did it again. We counted each one. By the time we left the hospital, he had sucked 52 times on a nipple by himself while the gavage tube was inserted through his nose, into the esophagus and then into his stomach. I was relieved. Surely this was proof that things would normalize and all of this drama would subside.

I knew I needed to be polite and go along with all the chaos, until things settled down and we could just go home. I tried my best to listen to what the doctors told me. Toward the end of the week, we were asked to choose a primary physician. We asked each of the doctors a few questions. The main questions on my mind were: "What will Zachary's life be like?" "What will our life be like?" "What can we do during this next year?"

Each doctor was compassionate and kind. Each time they answered our questions, I just smiled and nodded because I couldn't hear what they were saying.

The young male pediatrician who had admitted Zachary that first awful night asked me, "What do you want to do in this next year?"

What came out of my mouth surprised me: "If he only has a few months to live, then we want to take him to the east coast to see the autumn leaves. We want to take him on great hikes and show him the ocean." His simple question opened up new perspective. In that moment we came together as a young family and great doctor, to start building the blueprint for our life.

Zachary was hospitalized for eight days, and I left his side only for personal emergencies like a full bladder. Jonathan rotated between the hospital and taking care of things at home. His family flew in from Iowa, and mine came from New Jersey. Each of us tried to find new ways to be together, with grief lingering over us like a guillotine. The night before being discharged from the hospital, I wrote a simple ceremony. I left the title blank, though it felt like Zachary's funeral service. I handwrote a small program with songs, poems, and some personal insights I'd had during our intense hospitalization. As our discharge date got closer, I felt awkward carrying this funeral service in my bag, so the night before discharge, I renamed it "Zachary's Tree Ceremony."

A nurse made copies of my little handwritten program, and we ordered a tree from the local nursery and had it delivered to our home. My sister graciously called people to tell them we were coming home. We drove up the driveway to find 50–60 people mingling outside between the Russian olive trees and our home. People organically self-organized to plant Zachary's fifteen-foot ash tree and took turns holding him. I was tremendously relieved that I didn't need to talk much. I needed to be in a safe place where it was okay to not know myself or my future. The quiet gathering of familiar faces created a tremendous moment of safety for me. Then, without a lot of pomp and circumstance, we slowly gathered in a circle. Someone handed out the hand-written programs. We passed Zachary slowly around the circle and stumbled through the funeral service now converted to a ceremony of life.

My early days as the mom of a newborn were both effortless and exhausting. Despite his diagnosis, Zachary was an easy baby because he did not demand very much. He was quiet. I felt relieved that all the scary diagnoses were not obvious to me, and I was glad to be away from the intensity of loud beeps, introductions to new staff on each shift, and living in a single room. I also felt disoriented in multiple ways that I couldn't explain. It was as if I had been catapulted from Earth to another planet in a galaxy far away. It was easy to go through all the papers and stuff them in a paper bag to look at in another lifetime. I threw away the 1-800-epilepsy phone number because I didn't have any interest in joining a support group of people with problems.[3] I found a Jonathan Deer calendar and hand-wrote a bunch of medical appointments. Zachary was scheduled to attend physical therapy, occupational therapy, a metabolic disorder clinic in Denver, and a thrombosis clinic in Denver. Zachary, the baby, was easy to be with. Zachary's calendar of appointments replaced any newborn/toddler social life I had originally dreamed of.

By mid-September, I felt surprisingly comfortable suggesting the three of us go see a movie. I needed some way to normalize our life, and this felt like a no-brainer way for us to fit back into the world for 90 minutes. It would be our first big adventure and get our lives back on track. We looked at the matinees playing and picked one that wouldn't be too loud or scary to Zachary. The movie playing just happened to be **The Doctor** with William Hurt. It was a story of a doctor who had it all. He was successful, rich and had no problems.... until he was diagnosed with throat cancer. Throughout the movie he experienced medicine, hospitals, and doctors from a new perspective, the patient's perspective. He came to realize that there is more to being a doctor than surgery and prescriptions.

---

[3] Zachary had his first febrile seizure at home on the couch where his eyes rolled and his arms stiffened. He groaned loud for such a little boy. His skin turned bluish, and his body jerked rhythmically. I worried whatever was happening might kill him.

I felt comfortable in the dark theatre. The subject matter seemed comfortably familiar. We could pull out our stethoscope and gavage-feed Zachary his fluid in the dark movie theatre and not miss a thing. Life had already begun developing a "new normal." I was reaching for my old life and could almost grasp it.

During our first year together, I went through a lot of motions without emotion. We showed up on time to medical appointments and walked out with an EEG report weighing 6.5 pounds. Zachary's seizures were continuing to increase, and one way I handled it was to take a lot of photos so that I could remember the one precious year we had with him.[4] I took photos of ordinary moments—taking a bath in the sink, sitting in the grass, and walking to the mailbox so that I could remember him forever. I took photos of putting Zachary in a sled and sliding down the hill of our front yard. It was 31 degrees at sunset, and the sky was glowing pink. I was wearing blue jeans and a cream-colored cable-knit sweater; Zachary was wearing a powder-blue newborn snowsuit and a chunky white hat with a giant pom-pom on top. The snow was up to my knees. It was just the three of us outside in the silence trying to find our way. I was trying to grab moments that felt normal so that I could string them together and create some sense of being a family.

---

[4]   As Zachary's seizures increased in frequency, I also noticed they looked different. Some seizures were convulsive (stiffening and/or jerking variety), and some were on-convulsive (those with alter attention/ staring but no scary stiffening/ jerking). Some seizures lasted 5 seconds, some lasted longer than 20 minutes, and sometimes they came in clusters of 3 or 4 in a row. I caught myself often discounting this part of Zachary's diagnosis, the same way I would ignore the weeds in a garden. I didn't cope well embracing my feelings of sadness and grief. I often cut off from these feelings and would give Zachary medication and then go for a brisk walk with him to normalize my view of our world.

Friends with newborns the same age as Zachary stopped by our home in the country. The babies were young enough that differences weren't obvious, and our friends were kind in holding Zachary and showing deep compassion. As the winter began to melt, the pastures started to turn green. I don't know why, though during my pregnancy, I had visions of wearing matching outfits with my baby. My mother-in-law offered to make a few onesies for Zachary and matching shorts and short dresses for me. Zachary and I wore them all the time that first spring—Zachary in his navy blue onesie with little white anchors and white elastic trim and me in matching shorts and a white tank top. Another was made of tropical vibrant colors in bold geometric shapes. The fabric was soft, and many afternoons when I was too exhausted to drive to town, Zachary and I would lie outside in the weeds, Zachary on top of my chest wearing his boldly colored onesie to match my dress. I could feel our heartbeats beating together, and I practiced memorizing the moment.

Zachary loved animals and showed it by smiling: his whole body smiled. His face made a similar look when he was seizing, so sometimes I did take photos when he was having a seizure. My film camera had a delay from the time I clicked until the time it took the photo, and Zachary's head was usually bobbing when he smiled, so I just grabbed any photo I could of him smiling: seizure or seizure free.

Easter Sunday, 1991, Zachary was nine months old. He was wearing a little blue denim jacket and jeans, and he was bright eyed and happy. My sister had visited with her white angora fluffy bunny, and Zachary was totally animated. I noticed how it was easier for him to connect with someone or something sitting at eye level with him, in part because it was hard for him to hold his head up, let alone tilt his whole head to look up. During this weekend, however, he had a seizure that we could not stop.

The medical team at our local hospital was able to stop his seizure and monitor his breathing until he stabilized.

In mid-August, the week before his first birthday, I had planned a party. Actually, I had been planning his 1st birthday party ever since he got the prognosis of one year to live.

As his birthday approached, I stitched together a 3' × 4' flag with Zachary's name and a cartoon-like fabric character I made of him. I bought the sparklers, and then on August 29th, the day before his birthday, Zachary had a life-threatening status epileptic seizure. The doctors gave him a combination of benzodiazepines and phenytoin and monitored him in the ICU. There was talk about air-lifting him to another hospital; the doctors consulted with pediatric neurologists out of state. One brochure I found said that 30% of people who have status epilepticus are dead within 30 days. Zachary survived because of the physicians and nurses who were there. I would later learn of the incredible capacity of physicians who work wholeheartedly and communicate so powerfully through their own capacity to get real.

I felt too exhausted to re-schedule Zachary's birthday party. I was afraid I would burn out our friends by asking too much of them. I didn't want to invite people and then experience my own fear of no one coming. I didn't want to face my fear that the rest of the world was marching forward. I avoided any opportunity to admit that we might be forgotten.

So, I baked a life-sized cake and sheepishly knocked on our neighbors' door to ask if they might be willing to come over for 10 minutes and eat cake. I took a photo of the cake, a sparkler, four people and Zachary. I needed to tell myself that we were going to be okay.

CHAPTER 2

BIRTH AND NEW HOPES

During the winter of 1992, early in Zachary's second year, I poured a lot of energy into my life, yet I was empty. When I tried to talk or write about my feelings, I felt crazy. I wasn't writing about Zachary's disability; I was writing about a void in my life. I felt rudder-less and ashamed to say anything aloud. So I poured myself into being outdoors with Zachary. That cold Colorado winter, Jonathan attached a small purple toddler tub to an old sled. I dressed Zachary in a bright blue, red, and orange snowsuit and propped him with blankets shaped like tootsie rolls. It took us 20 minutes to get ready, 20 minutes to walk down to the mailbox, 20 minutes to walk back. It wasn't about getting the mail; it was about me and my 15-month-old baby getting outside together just once each day. I didn't have any internal compass to tell if I was being a good mom or a bad mom, so my default was to feel like I was failing. When we were outside, however, I was able to quiet the noise in my head and the chaos in my heart. Being outside and walking paused the darkness that was pouring through a funnel into my soul.

I did feel a sense of connection with some women I had met in Fort Collins—Julie Schleusener was another mom of four children, and her baby had been labeled with disabilities We had our first conversation in the middle of a parking lot after a meeting at the DisAbility Connection; Carol was a part of the Newcomer's group we joined when we had first moved there. She had a way of seeing people in ways they didn't even fully see themselves. Lisa attended the same church we did and walked her faith by sticking her hand way out and offering to do things like watch Zachary overnight. By the end of the long winter, I had an idea to arrange a tea party in the backyard for these friends as well as some other moms of young kids, toddlers, and babies. I sent out homemade invitations and on the afternoon of the tea party felt relieved when six women arrived with their children. The moms and young girls wore dresses with floral prints and hats accented with netting and contrasting bows. Everyone sat in the grass with Zachary in his blue sailor suit. I cut sandwiches into triangles, and other people brought small hors d'oeuvres. I served iced tea from a blue-and-white Hadley pottery pitcher and felt in that moment that we belonged.

JMT Company (the company was named after Jonathan's initials) did not end up generating any revenue, so Jonathan interviewed for a job and went back to work in Loveland. We divided and conquered the work of raising a family. We still didn't express affection to each other, though we both adored Zachary. We agreed we wanted more children and, based upon initial testing, learned there were not any obvious genetic concerns. One physician mentioned the chances of having another child with similar complexities would be like lightning striking the same spot in our backyard the size of a postage stamp. Jonathan and I didn't need to talk about the topic much. He grew up in a family of four kids, and I have three siblings, all of us close in age. So, with minimal conversation, we had a cordial agreement to continue growing our family.

In October of 1992, I was thirty years old and pregnant with our second baby. The pregnancy felt easy, and I was having moments of "normalcy."

This time, however, I didn't have the energy to look through baby books and daydream about the future. I was holding Zachary, measuring medications, scheduling medical appointments, gavage-feeding him through a tube, or ignoring the fact that I had a lot to learn about the different kinds of seizures Zachary was having.

I had received the message loud and clear that Zachary had severe cerebral palsy. I'd heard other scary labels describing his other disabilities, though I ignored terms like mental retardation, developmental delays. If I put attention on all of his medical issues, I would slide down a dark rabbit hole of a despair and never find my way out.

So, I flipped through all the brochures about agencies and organizations that could teach us about seizures. Then I threw them away. Instead, I scribbled notes on pieces of paper when Zachary would stiffen and arch his back. I would hold him tight when his entire body violently jerked from head to toe. I made mental notes of when one side of his body would sporadically jolt, lurch, and shake in his car seat while we were driving. At a graduation party in Longmont one afternoon, I noticed Zachary looked so peaceful gazing into the woods, only to find out this was another type of seizure, called absence seizure. I felt comfortable talking with his pediatric neurologist about this, though the idea of joining a support group completely overwhelmed me.

The idea of having another baby gave me a sense of hope that we could recalibrate our lives to blend medical appointments with visits to the park and story hour at the library. As our delivery date got closer, we wanted to know if she was a girl or if he was a boy. The ultrasound showed he was a boy, which made everything feel more real. We narrowed down his name to Hunter, Clarence, or Taylor.

Unlike Zachary's birth, where my water broke at home and his delivery was drug-free, my obstetrician had scheduled an induction. Taylor appeared to be big. As I walked in the door of the hospital, I asked, "Do you promise to give me an epidural?" The nurses assured me this was in my plan, and the records show that it was administered, though it did not minimize any of the pain. Once I was in active labor, the insides of my entire body twisted, pulled, squeezed with intense waves of raw pain. By the time Taylor's head came out, I was exhausted.

"Stop pushing," the nurse said. Then, "One more push and his body would pop out."

I pushed. I pushed again. The doctor looked straight into my eyes, and I felt I was being scolded. "Your baby's shoulders are bigger than his head. You have two chances to push him out, otherwise we will break his clavicle, fold his shoulders toward his chin, and pull him out."

I roared like a mama bear protecting my baby from imminent threat. I moaned as my baby boy squeezed out of me and into the bright lights of the noisy, sterile room.

Taylor Robert Scott was born on June 14, 1993. He was 9 lbs. 11 oz., and his foot was so big the print of his five chubby toes went off the page. He latched on quickly to nurse and by six months weighed 24 pounds from nursing alone.

But in those few weeks after Taylor's birth, I was struggling. Taylor had colic and would cry uncontrollably for hours at a time. He clenched his fingers, arched his back and kicked his legs. I was either too naïve to imagine this could be related to seizure activity or too exhausted to consider the idea. I took him to the doctor and was assured that I just needed to keep him well fed, in clean diapers, and burped. It was a difficult six weeks. I got up during the night to sit in the rocking chair, holding my babies, and silently cursed all the magazine covers of new moms wearing long, smooth, white lace nightgowns and looking like models at midnight. My milk was leaking, Taylor was crying, and I felt like my body was a science experiment.

Barbara Stutsman was the director of a local agency, The DisAbility Connection, and a mom. During this time, she called, introduced herself, and asked if she could come to our home to meet Zachary. I couldn't imagine why she would want to do that, though she sounded quite nice, like she really wanted to meet our little boy. She drove to our home and held Zachary while I tried to comfort Taylor. In later visits, Barbara would bring her two daughters, Rachel and Esther, to visit us. While I tried to console Taylor, Barbara supported Rachel, Esther, and Zachary with the ease of a 21st-century shaman.

Barbara invited us to attend a conference hosted by the Colorado Department of Education, called Parents Encouraging Parents (PEP). She described her personal experience of how she and other families gathered support, information and education. It didn't appeal to me, though I trusted Barbara, and she truly believed we would be inspired.

Seeing our struggle, Barbara also offered to coordinate a new type of planning meeting for us. Actually, she offered it to all local families of kids with disabilities between birth and three years old. It was called an Individualized Family Support Plan (IFSP). The gist of it was to gather the people we valued and organize a conversation about our dreams, hopes, and needs to live a meaningful life as a family.

I didn't realize until later that a new public policy was just being put in place. The policy was called 1993 Senate Bill 1085, and, simply put, it made sure babies with disabilities could be treated like babies and supported like babies doing baby-like things. Before the passing of this law, babies with disabilities would be treated like small adults. In other words, they would be treated in adult settings on adult schedules focused on specific challenges through the mindset of an adult. This public policy provided funding to imagine childlike ways and innovative approaches to support babies with disabilities and families in ways that were meaningful at this stage of their life. The principles of the IFSP were:

- Understanding of how the early years are the foundation for a child's healthy development and readiness for lifelong learning.

- Services must be child-centered.

- Programs should be family-focused.

- Programs should be culturally sensitive.

- Collaborative interagency coordination is the most efficient and effective way to provide services to families.

- Programs should provide transdisciplinary approaches.

I had never heard of such a thing. The way Barbara talked about it, we could invite the people we wanted and get input about our strengths as a family. We could talk about our hopes and dreams for Zachary and seek encouragement and ideas about how to go about the next chapter of our lives by leveraging everyday people and places.

I made invitations and sent them to friends, family, and providers who were working directly with Zachary. Making homemade invitations was a practical way for me to fulfill a yearning to creatively express myself more publicly. They were also a way for me to think about people and send them a small, personalized message. I baked cookies and small snacks. I couldn't tell if this was a formal meeting or a party, so I decided to consider this a party-like event with music and an agenda. I was nervous that no one would come. I was nervous that people *would* come and not know what to say. I was nervous that people would say anything.

Barbara's vision was to host a dynamic process that could help us utilize natural resources in the community that I did not even know were out there. Because I was busy trying to re-invent my sense of self and understanding of who we were as a family, I had ignored the fact that the world around me was humming and buzzing and carrying on.

As the meeting got closer, I had a change of heart and didn't want to do it. I told Barbara about some of my fears and concerns. Actually, I told her a lot of things that I felt ashamed to say aloud. I felt ashamed that I couldn't think of hopes for Zachary. The only things I could imagine for him were visions of isolation and our family pretending like everything was okay. The only reason I was coping in the moment was because all babies were dependent upon their families in similar ways as Zachary.

Barbara said I wouldn't need to say anything. She and the person who would facilitate the meeting would lead the discussion. I could simply listen.

The day came, and people came. I had been afraid people would offer a polite reason for not coming, and I would feel bad for even asking them to come and then be reminded of how lonely our life was. Instead, here they were. We had rented a small room at an apartment clubhouse in Fort Collins with a fireplace. I set out the food and turned on a radio station with top 100 *Billboard* songs. It almost felt like a party, where it was going to be okay if I smiled. Zachary's physician, occupational therapist, physical therapist, and other professionals came. We had also invited some friends whom I had cut off from a bit, and family. We even took a risk and invited two families from church whom I wanted to like, though I just hadn't gotten the gumption to reach out and introduce myself. There was something about them that was so approachable I decided to just go with it.

The meeting was conversational. Barbara and Terri, a CSU professor and board member of the DisAbility Connection, hosted an open dialogue. People were invited to bring "all of themselves" and were simultaneously invited to speak about "all of Zachary and all of our family." It was so different from what I had expected. We discussed problems that seemed mundane but could make big differences in our lives. I had not been able to find a stroller that could support both Zachary and Taylor's bodies. We were struggling to figure out if we should move into a more wheelchair-accessible home or start making modifications to our current home that we loved. Since leaving my corporate job and jumping into the world of disabilities, I didn't even know where moms of babies and toddlers spent time. I couldn't figure out who or how to ask: "Where do moms and babies connect and meet one another?" I felt like the rest of the world had a membership card to go spend time together, but I never got mine in the mail.

Zachary's physician, Dr. John Guenther, was also a dad and active in our community. He was an incredibly compassionate physician who created strong connections with folks as people first. Dr. John G was a remarkable man who had the innate ability to be fully present in the moment, as if nothing else mattered. He would address sensitive subjects and express insights to others in ways that were useful and meaningful to them. He was aware of a Capstone construction program a few miles away at Colorado State University (CSU). He brainstormed aloud and wondered if the senior students in this program would be interested in meeting with us and writing a proposal about how to affordably adapt our home to be wheelchair accessible. As he spoke, he described a vision of how a CSU senior team could apply their construction-management skills to a real-world challenge (our home) and align it with the expectations the Capstone project required for graduation. He offered suggestions about other people and resources that could be creatively leveraged to match our needs. Up until this point, I had seen him only as a physician, though this new perspective of seeing him as a human and a dad opened up all kinds of conversations for us in later appointments.

Zachary's occupational therapist knew of a specific type of double stroller in which each of the individual seats could be removed and plopped on the ground at the park or anywhere. She painted a vision of how we didn't need to haul additional seating equipment around to support Zachary to sit in the outdoors. The energy and the conversation were attuned to our original visions of being a family. People discussed family activities, toddler classes at the rec center, story hour at the library. It was as if we could talk about people and families first, and all of the adaptations second.

I had no idea what could happen when we brought all of ourselves to a conversation. There was a sense of extreme intimacy. I felt hope.

I felt hope that I could read Zachary's emotions and provide him comfort and love, and feel a deep sense of connection for him in this world.

I felt hope that Taylor would experience his own sense of well-being and belonging as a baby and a brother.

I felt hope that Zachary and Taylor would stumble upon their own way of doing things together.

I felt hope that I didn't need to live a life of isolation.

CHAPTER 3

ADAPTING, ONE CONVERSATION AT A TIME

In an effort to reach out and be in the world, I volunteered with the DisAbility Connection as a Board member and also on a committee in Denver with the Colorado Interagency Coordinating Council. The CICC was a group of 35 leaders, each of whom was appointed by the governor that would advise the state agency how to implement the new policies within the Individuals with Disabilities Act (IDEA). I usually took the boys with me, so sometimes I wasn't even sure what the meeting was about. Barbara seemed to think I would have something to contribute, though my focus was just on practicing how to show up in places other than medical appointments without crying.

"Would you like to co-lead the Colorado Interagency Coordinating Council? It wouldn't be more than 10 or so hours a week." Elizabeth Hepp, who worked at the Colorado Department of Education, asked me. By this time in my life, I had pretty well mastered the polite look on the outside, while silently crying on the inside.

"Uh, thank you so much for asking but.... no way." I was making progress in life, but this would be too much. I could now empty the diaper bag every night, make sure we got outside for a walk daily, and I was even beginning to answer the phone when it rang. Elizabeth suggested I think about it and she would ask again. I thought she was crazy.

The following week, the boys and I visited the Denver children's museum. The boys were four and two years old, and I was poor at planning all the details, though capable of improvising our life. I didn't have a checklist or set of routines like the good mothers. I tended to walk through the house and pick up things I needed like spare shirts, extra diapers and baby wipes in case the ones I left in the car were dried up, a fist full of medications, pill crusher, different bottles for drinking, the special seat with straps to put inside Zachary's side of the double stroller, the Ziploc bag of leftover cereal and Gogurts in a small portable tote that I kept telling myself I would wipe out next time. Each morning routine started with me feeling completely inadequate. I knew what I knew, and I was in over my head. I felt like everyone else must have gotten a Mother's Handbook once discharged from the hospital, and I never got mine.

I looked for ways to funnel Taylor's energy, so pulling into the parking lot of the Denver museum, I asked him where he thought we ought to park. As we unloaded I asked Taylor to tell me what he could see in the parking lot. Sometimes I would ask if he could pose to match something he saw. As I unstrapped Zachary from his car seat and re-strapped him into his new seat in the stroller, I guessed what Taylor was imitating. Taylor was creative, curious, and active. He liked to talk, jump, pick up rocks, throw pinecones, and pose like a crooked pine tree. Zachary silently turned his head left and right to watch as Taylor played alongside of him. Taylor talked a lot, and I loved to ask him questions to nurture his independence, giving him a voice in his life and me a nanosecond to figure out the next step for Zachary's life. As we stood in line, I spotted a newsletter along the windowsill. It was from the Coaches Training Institute, and along the left column they listed the cornerstones of the organization. One of them was a belief that "all people are naturally creative, resourceful, and whole."

I felt something I had not felt before.

I felt a little, tiny something soften in my heart, for the first time.

I felt myself take a breath, and I actually felt my breath.

It was like someone had just turned the dial from a black/white to full color. I shoved the newsletter in the overstuffed diaper bag. I was desperately wondering if this could actually be true for Zachary, for Taylor, maybe even for me.

The next time I saw Elizabeth, at a CICC meeting in Denver, I mentioned this coach training was available. The Colorado Department of Education was the lead agency in Colorado responsible for the implementation of the new IDEA policies. One of the decisions CDE made as the lead agency was to select a parent of a child with a disability to partner with one of the 35 leaders to co-lead the CICC. Elizabeth, along with her team, was interested in developing leadership skills in parents of children with disabilities. I said, "If CDE would consider sending me to this training, I will do the 10-hours-per-week role." I assured her that I was a high-risk investment. I would probably fail and quite frankly thought she had picked the wrong person.

Luckily, Elizabeth saw something in me that I had no access to. The members of the DisAbility Connection were real people engaging in real conversations. I felt lucky that I was invited to hang out with them and call it a meeting. One member was David Pond. David and his wife Jennifer were the parents of a baby with Down syndrome, and David was a former tennis competitor. At one of the board meetings, the subject of fundraising came up. David had this vision of a family-oriented, community-wide tennis tournament as a fundraiser for the DisAbility Connection. His idea was to have athletes from a five-state region compete. Our tournament would be the first tennis tournament in Fort Collins to feature a wheelchair division! He sounded so convincing, and other Board members were on board.

I wondered if this activity could be fun. I wondered if one of these new people might become friends with me. Up until this point, I had lost all sense of fun, recreation, or friends. I was beginning to feel glimpses of buoyancy. Jonathan was not interested in attending the fundraiser, which did not surprise me. Our typical routine was to divide and conquer. I was beginning to think that even though I was struggling to find my own thoughts and feelings, I was able to find more oxygen in my life.

As parents and members of DisAbility Connections, we started to imagine that all kids could register to take any class offered by the Fort Collins Recreation Department. In April of 1995, we presented an inspirational vision to the Fort Collins City Council with a request for the city to add a line item on the city budget to hire a therapeutic recreational specialist. The presentation was a compilation of videos and stories of people with a wide range of significant disabilities water skiing, dancing, mountain climbing, and all sorts of crazy stuff. The key point was that there would not be separate classes, rather a city where any person could register for any recreation class. Our vision was to live in a city and offer recreational opportunities where staff would automatically say "yes" and then provide all adaptations. The city voted unanimously "yes," completed a national interview process, and hired Renee Lee, CTRS.

As soon as Renee was hired, I called the registration desk to sign Zachary up for the pre-school "Skate and Create" class. I had watched how other preschoolers went to this amazing three-hour program combining ice skating, swimming, snacks, and arts and crafts.

So at the age of five and in his first little wheelchair, I stood in the background and watched as Zachary was attached to a board with ice skates that Jonathan had made. Zachary then swam with the support of a volunteer and—this was the biggest surprise—during the arts and crafts activity, he was sitting in a small circle of other five-year-olds in his little adaptive chair on the floor, and the volunteer was sitting across from him between two other kids in the circle. I was so surprised because I thought the volunteer would be helicoptering around Zachary to help him. Instead, the volunteers were trained to support bigger visions—visions of allowing natural relationships to unfold in natural environments.

Norman Kunc, a well-known advocate for people with disabilities, introduced a model that resonated with me describing how relationships can't be mandated. He described how relationships are more magical than that. In fact, he suggested that relationships are two parts proximity and one part chemistry. In other words, you've got to be hanging out in places with other like-minded souls, to then allow chemistry to happen, or not happen.

It took me a while to understand how natural community begins to reveal itself. By having a volunteer whose purpose was to support a great learning experience for all the kids, she was focused on the big picture and allowing the two parts proximity/one part chemistry thing to unfold.

I was beginning to feel a deep and authentic awareness of how we could live our family in a new way. We would not be the family I had hoped for and dreamed of. We would not be the broken family always isolated and feeling like the outcast. We could start living our lives one day at a time and one conversation at a time.

While Taylor was occupied with talking, exploring, talking, walking, and talking, Zachary was attending our neighborhood kindergarten and fully engaged in ordinary activities. I had been avoiding literature about disabilities, support groups about disabilities, social workers who helped families with disabilities. I had worked hard to figure out how to fit in with the world though I knew it was becoming more and more obvious that Zachary was very different from other kindergarteners. The other children in his class had all learned the eight activities of daily living: Use the toilet, eat, dress, bathe, groom, get out of bed, get out of a chair, and walk. In fact, Zachary wore diapers, was spoon fed pureed food, needed to be dressed, needed to be supported while washing him in a tub, needed someone to position him on his side in bed and roll him over during the night to prevent bedsores on his body, lift him in and out of each chair and use assorted straps depending upon the time of day to help hold him in molded chairs, and adjust cushions/seats to get around from place to place. Zachary also needed a 24/7 line-of-sight supervision because some of his seizures were silent, and some involved an abrupt burst of screaming that sounded like a scene in a horror movie when someone was unexpectedly about to be murdered alone at midnight in the woods.

Even so, I was hopeful there were some nice people who could see Zachary as a young boy first and a disability second.

He attended Shepardson Elementary. The principal knew each of the kids by name, and the teachers were a step ahead of me. Kids were curious and took turns pushing him and his little purple wheel chair when they walked down the hallway in two straight lines. Mr. Sheets, the physical education teacher, adapted the gym class so everyone was included. Zachary had a paraprofessional assigned to him, though she deliberately arranged herself to build connections between the kids rather than helicopter around Zachary. When kids asked what Zachary was thinking, Mr. Sheets would say, "I don't know. Let's ask him." Kids would ask Zachary, then the paraprofessional would ask, "What do you notice?" Kids began to create meaning with each other. Zachary was included in circle time, and when it was his turn, someone would help him push the big red button on his Dynavox—a clunky, heavy device bolted to his wheelchair onto which we would record a message each morning about what he did at home the night before. A loud robotic voice would mechanically speak a new message each morning: "I. Helped. My. Brother. Fold. Laundry. And. Then. We. Watched. Toy. Story. Two." in a monotone voice. As he left kindergarten each day, the paraprofessional would invite one of Zachary's peers to notice something Zachary had done and then record the message, so that Zachary could hit the big red button when he got home and we could chat about what he had done that day.

Sometimes it was easy to generate adaptions. Sometimes it was exhausting. Sometimes it felt authentic while other moments were mechanical and cumbersome. It was tricky for me to figure out which part of establishing relationships was awkward because of Zachary's disability and which part of establishing relationships was cumbersome just because relationships take time and energy. It seemed like so much of life was naturally awkward that I wanted to discern which parts of life were part of ordinary life and which parts of life were extra complicated because of Zachary. The relationships which felt most comfortable were with people who seemed to be comfortable in their own skin. Some of these people were friends, physicians, and strangers on the street. Other relationships were strained and painful and seemed to be with people who were so busy helping us that we felt "less than" them.

In April, Lindsey Pointer invited four girls and three boys to her Easter-themed birthday party—Zachary's first. As Zachary sat in his chair, all eight children were the same height. Zachary was plopped in the middle of the outdoor birthday activities, and I was surrounded by moms talking about all the unexpected trials of parenthood: "Erin cut her own bangs right down to the root!" I could feel the iron gates around my heart soften. I experimented for a moment with how motherhood could be a little more about being human together.

CHAPTER 4

DEAR JOHN LETTER

Jonathan and I were increasingly living parallel lives. The irony is that Zachary's diagnosis was not the thing driving us apart.[5] We simply had never really connected. My marriage was not right, and I was struggling to understand why. I had been raised to go to college, marry someone from the Midwest, find a job, and then leave my job to raise a family. According to my family upbringing, I was right on track.

According to something deeper, I was suffocating. The more I denied these feelings, the more embarrassed I became. As I did begin to reach out to a counselor and two older women at church, I realized this emptiness would probably only be addressed in three ways. Jonathan and I could continue seeing a counselor and resolve the emptiness. We could continue to live separate but parallel lives. Or we could get divorced.

---

[5] Depending on the type of study one may read on disability and divorce, that which drives parents of a child with a disability apart is usually NOT the disability but instead deeper issues that can often be magnified by disagreements over the disability. Aside from couples having a child with severe non-verbal autism, the divorce rate of couples having one or more disabled children is LESS than those with non-disabled children: 40% vs 50–60% respectively. The pain, anguish, and shared meaning of raising a child with a disability seemingly adds to the meaning of a marriage, fostering it.

Instead of a one-part tragedy, I was about to enter a darker and even lonelier tragedy. At the heart of the clash, I could not discern who I was and how to take a stand for myself. I did not feel prepared to live on my own with two children. I was not prepared to chart a future alone for Zachary's life. I had no energy to build up a mask of optimism and hope. I was consumed with guilt and shame that I could not mold myself to fit into this marriage.

The couple's counselor we were seeing agreed that we were not compatible. The lack of emotional connection was obvious. We did not express affection in romantic ways, and our counselor said that marriage is intended to be more than a business partnership. As the topic of separating came up, I panicked and asked the counselor, "Don't you think those scenes in movies where people look at each other with soft eyes is a bunch of Hollywood baloney?"

His reply: "Couples do feel connections like that, and it can be real." I left each appointment feeling more discouraged that I didn't even know what he was talking about.

Not long after this session, seemingly out of nowhere, Jonathan made an announcement. I was standing in the kitchen between the dark green wall filled with the boys' framed artwork and the kitchen island. Jonathan came walking out of the office into the hallway.

After a prolonged silence, I asked, "Are you mad at me?"

"I am not going to keep working at ESI."

Silence.

"Um...."

"You can keep the house, the money in the bank accounts, and the boys. I need a car. You can have the rest. I am leaving and going back to Iowa."

Jonathan left early the next morning. Upon his return a week later, we mutually agreed to divorce. Without any discussion, Jonathan went to the County Courthouse and filed a petition. We didn't talk about the process and I didn't know what to expect, so I pretended I wasn't shaking when an older man knocked on the door.

"You are being formally served a divorce petition which has been filed by Jonathan Mark Turner at the Larimer County Courthouse."

"Oh."

"The documents outline the decree and dissolution of marriage. Please sign and date here to acknowledge you have received these documents."

I opened the large envelope and saw my name listed below Jonathan's. He was the petitioner. I was the respondent. And a new reality began.

The legal and financial issues were cumbersome and scary to me, not to mention the emotional ramifications, trips back and forth to court to settle ongoing custody, child support, and other issues. I was also weighted with these horrible fears of how I would ever find health insurance and what other people would think of me.

When waves of fear and shame washed over me, I cried to the point of exhaustion. Sometimes I would drive north on I-25 past the Colorado state line to a rest area with big dinosaur rocks. The parking lot was always empty, and so was the massive windy Wyoming landscape all around— brown, bald, and barren. It reflected the emptiness and hollowness I felt inside. I hated the feeling of isolation, and I wondered if I would ever find a way to come up for air and belong in the world again. I couldn't talk about this internal death sentence with anyone, so I didn't. I had gone from avoiding my feelings after Zachary's birth, to experiencing a wide range of depressing emotions, and now divorcing myself from the world during the early stages of my separation.

I scheduled an appointment with my physician to get a physical exam before being removed from Jonathan's insurance. On the morning of my appointment, I packed up Zachary's wheelchair, his diapers, and medication. I packed Taylor a snack and dropped him off at a friend's house. Taylor was an energetic, walking, talking three-year-old, and he needed to be in a place where he could play. As Zachary and I entered the doctor's office, I told them it would be my last physical with this doctor and explained I would be changing health insurance. I burst into tears and said I was getting divorced. The woman at the front desk escorted Zachary and me back to a patient room immediately. Dr. Burnham, my physician, walked in and sat beside me on a small rolling chair. She didn't say a word, and I cried harder. As I sobbed, Zachary started to giggle. Whenever I cried, sneezed, farted, or burped, Zachary giggled.

Dr. Burnham listened. I told her that I didn't want any conflict and I was scared about the next steps in my life. I did not have a plan. She listened some more and then asked me to put on the gown and said she would return to do my physical. As she walked out, she asked if Zachary could sit at the front desk with the business manager. I agreed, and she wheeled him out of my exam room. When she returned, she asked me to lie down. She said she would be back in an hour and that I needed to rest. I started to cry again and explained I did not have time to do this and begged her to just do my exam. She nodded, smiled, gently closed the door, and walked away.

I lay there feeling angry that she was wasting my time. I struggled to breathe and was flooded with emotions of more shame and guilt. All the voices in my head reminded me of what people were going to think of me. How could I walk away from a nice home, stable relationship, and all the makings of an ideal American life? What would people at church think? What would my friends think? How could I unpack all the lies I had told myself about my life?

I lay on my back, consumed with fear of the future. The "shoulds" in my head got louder and louder. The one thing I could do was at least be kind to Jonathan through the divorce process. I would not hire an attorney and would trust that we could figure this out together in a friendly way. This thought comforted me.

When Dr. Burnham walked back in to do my physical, she was deeply present with me and spoke quietly. "You will need to hire an attorney." She explained that women typically begin a divorce process wanting to be kind and connecting, only to find out years later, when living close to poverty, that they did not stand up for themselves. As the appointment came to a close, she asked me to sing a song aloud. I couldn't think of a song. She went and got Zachary, brought him back into the room, and asked me again. I said I knew all the words to the *Lion King*. She said, "Good. Let's sing it aloud." Next, she pulled out a prescription pad and wrote five items:

1. Sing aloud each day.

2. Shop the perimeter of the grocery store and eat foods that come out of the ground.

3. Dance, walk, or discover another movement you like, and do it daily.

4. Call an attorney.

5. Take Prozac for 90 days, and ask one girlfriend if she notices a difference.

Two days later, Dr. Burnham called our home. She said it was a follow-up phone call and asked if I was following my five prescriptions. I said I could do some of them. She asked if I had called an attorney. It was like I was hearing her for the first time. "No." I did not want any conflict during our divorce. She said, "I understand, but for the health and well-being of your children, you need to do this." This time I heard her.

One of my biggest challenges was to find a place for the three of us to live that I could afford. Jonathan was going to return from Iowa and stay in the house until it would be put on the market and sold. Eventually, the house sold, he moved into an apartment, and then he bought another home. When I asked the boys what was important to them, Taylor said he wanted a basketball hoop at our house. Zachary did not use words, though I was aware of how much vitality he could access when he swam, so walking distance to a recreation center would be optimal. My one wish was to have room were we could put our fig tree. For whatever reason, being near a tree gave me comfort.

Our friend, Barb Stutsman, had spotted a small condo at 1808 Centennial Road in Fort Collins, so that Friday afternoon, Zachary, Taylor, and I rang the doorbell and asked for information. We didn't exactly walk through the place, though we got the price and said we would call them Monday.

In the meantime, I quickly visited four banks. Three of them said they would not give me a loan. The fourth banker said they would offer me a loan, though it would include extra points and be set at a higher interest rate because I did not have a full-time job. I was thrilled and made an offer on the house the following Monday only to find out they had received another offer for the full asking price.

All of the noise in my head went silent. I felt a sense of laying myself down. I knew that I did have a meaningful relationship with my two young boys, and I was gaining enough oxygen that I could create a bubble to shield them so they could expand within this bubble and not feel my fear of the world.

The next day, we got a call. To this day, I don't know why, but the owners had made a decision to sell the condo to the three of us. On Tuesday, June 2, I put on a white blouse with a big white collar buttoned to the top. I wore a black skirt, curled my hair, and went alone to the bank to close on the loan. By Friday, David, Barbara, and others helped me move out of the newly built, wheelchair-accessible home Jonathan and I had built and into 1808 Centennial Road, David and another friend mounted a basketball hoop above the garage door and moved the fig tree from the old house into the living room of our condo. Oh—and did I mention we would now live across the street from a small neighborhood pool?

The move into our new condo had given me a respite from the dark night of the soul. I now felt a hint of some breathing space as I started feeling connected to our new home and our new life. We were heading into winter, though, and the short days.

The boys were sharing a room with a monitor so I could manage Zachary's seizure activity. We had a small kitchen with a table to share meals, open mail, pay bills, and entertain each other. I did not have much discretionary money, and I did not want my kids to think that we were poor. Jonathan did pay alimony and child support, though I was scraping by. So, in moments like this, my "millions of good ideas" were of use to me. I went to Wal Mart and bought 100 tea light candles for $2.99. I hid them randomly in drawers, plants, pots, pans, laundry, pantry, garage, etc. After school I told the boys to find as many as they could. Then, I would start figuring out what the heck we would have for dinner.

By the time they found candles, I would start making dinner. Then, we would light some, eat, do dishes, take baths, read a very-very-short book and voila: I could tell myself we were a family and we would survive. The only other options were to cry, drink, or go to bed when it got dark at 4:45PM.

Crying was a good option. Drinking was not, because I never knew when we'd be going to the ER to get help in stopping Zachary's seizures. Going to bed at 4:45PM was also a good option. We discovered Dr. Phil, so sometimes we would lie on the bed at 4:30 to watch the second half of his show.

Scavenger hunts for tea lights and eating by candlelight turned out to be an okay option to manage the very long nights in our first winter at 1808 Centennial Road.

Note to reader: My editor asked me to address my feelings during this time in my life, and I struggled to figure out what to write. I decided to just sit down in front of my computer and "show up to the page." I put my fingers on the keyboard to type the first word. Any word. The words turned into a letter, and below are the exact words I wrote. No edits were made.

Dear John,

You asked to me to marry you and I said yes. I did my best, and I failed. I did my best to see our differences as ways to complete each other, and I know we both tried. Yet I failed.

You agreed we could go on adventures together, even though you preferred to be at home to garden and work in the workshop alone. Before we had kids, you acknowledged my passion to explore the world and agreed we could go as a couple.

We planned a B&B trip to New England in the autumn, though I only remember you wanting to watch TV in a hotel room. We visited the Cotswold Villages of England to walk the rural landscape of stately homes and fairytale gardens, though we sat in silence on the flight over and back. We bought matching motorcycles and took weekend road trips to explore Taos to the south and our neighboring states. As we talked in the evenings, you focused on the logistics; I was busy absorbing the new sights, sounds, and smells. I ached to experience more of this in our relationship, though I couldn't figure out how to bring any sensuality to our marriage.

We had endless trials and errors. I know there were times I came on too strong. I would tell you my flights of ideas as they came to me, and I could have filtered myself. I took long periods of silence personally and thought you were angry or disappointed with me most of the time.

I tried my best to listen to your needs. I know you wanted to live in the country. I had no experience living in the country, though I tried. I hope you know that. I know you liked to do things in private and avoid crowds, so I tried to find hobbies that we could do alone as a couple. I thought the tandem bicycle was a good idea, though we only rode it three times.

I heard you say that you wanted me to go to bed with you and wake up with you, though the miles between us for months at a time was more painful than keeping myself busy and feeling the distance. I wasn't avoiding you in the mornings, though we lacked any sense of intimacy or affection, so I got up early to go walk before the boys woke up.

I knew that quality time is crucial for any marriage, and I searched myself to figure out how we could be together, without the temptation to do tasks. We would sit in silence at meals. We would work in silence in the yard together. I would bring you a glass of water when you were doing a project outside in the sun. I don't know if those things made a difference.

I felt ignored. I felt like it was difficult for you to tolerate me. One day I asked if you liked anything about me. There was a long pause, even by an introvert's standards. Eventually you said, "You are creative," though it was with the same tone of voice someone else might say, "Look at the weed in the sidewalk."

I could not read you, and the harder I tried, the more I pushed us apart. I tried to bring the Midwestern values I learned as a little girl to our marriage, though some of the lessons I grew up with no longer seem relevant. I found it hard to explain to you that I was capable of creating our life together, though I needed to feel like we had each other's back. I needed to know that you got me and understood me. I wanted to be part of your inner life, not just the business of setting up a home. I felt like there were so many plans and rules to live by. There was a lack of any flexibility, fun, or pleasure.

Each of us love the boys, and we were able to successfully adapt our lives to meet their needs. You sorted, organized, and managed the insurance of Zachary's medical bills. You played with both of the boys in the evenings and helped with their care. But it was exhausting for me to live a separate and parallel life to you. The sadness I feel is bottomless. I am sad we never found a way to let down our guard and truly collaborate in building our life together.

Sandy

The judge legally signed my divorce on September 10, 1998, exactly seven years to the day Zachary was diagnosed with severe brain damage.

PART II

Zachary & Taylor sitting in back yard at 1808 Centennial Rd.

CHAPTER 5

LIFE AT 1808

Soon, the long nights turned into spring. We did not have much, but it was enough. We bought a lilac bush and planted it in front of the boys' bedroom window next to the basketball hoop. In 1997, we had secured assistance from the Children's Extensive Services waiver, which paid for people like Jared and Michelle to help support Zachary. Jared was 6'2" and wore a choker of shells around his neck. He had played basketball all his life and took care of Zachary like a 210-pound teddy-bear. Michelle was a curly haired blonde nursing student at UNC and was gifted with ambition, drive, and compassion. The two of them rotated shifts, and, together, we began to find our way into the first spring season in our new home. Jonathan had the boys half the time, and although were each allowed to share the CES benefit 50/50, he declined, as he did not want people in his house.

Some days I felt hopeful. Some days I stared at the clock and just wanted to go to bed. Once, when I was feeling particularly isolated, I called my good friend Julie to tell her that I was not going to be able to meet her at Warren Park. Zachary was having too many seizures. He looked floppy, and I felt lifeless. She said okay and hung up. An hour later, Julie knocked on the front door. She was holding a lawn chair and an Oprah magazine. She said, "No need to even notice I am here. I am going to sit in the backyard. I have a magazine and can entertain myself or play with the boys. You can ignore me, and then I'll leave in about an hour." I felt relieved that I wasn't alone. At least for this afternoon.

Some parts of my life were limping along slowly. I had earned $786 in 1997 and was on track to earn $25,340 with my work as the CICC Co-chair and at the Disability Connection in 1998. This felt grim, though I didn't really have many options. Zachary's seizure activity would escalate at unexpected times, so I always felt tentative about making or sometimes following through on plans. I also struggled with my own confidence in finding a job or career path where I could meet my kids' needs as a single mom and support us. I knew of another single parent going back into the workforce by getting an entry-level job at JC Penney's. But I couldn't imagine balancing a sales job at the mall with my children's needs. I couldn't imagine having enough job security as a life coach to pay my bills. I did feel a sense of hope that some kind of clarity would emerge if I diligently stayed on top of my coach training program. The CDE reimbursed the expenses for me to attend the 15 days of basic training, which I was grateful for. The fundamental coursework was five courses, three days each, which took me about nine months to complete.

When we moved to the condo, I was in the early stages of beginning the fundamental training program. (Later I would go on to complete the six-month certification program, which was a separate rigorous training course that focused on advanced skill development, supervision, and oral and written exams. I also would attend the one-year Leadership Program designed to integrate coaching skills into leadership roles (versus one-on-one coaching relationships). As I got started, I needed a place to organize my files, notes, documentation for training purposes, and do my coaching calls. In order to complete my coach certification,

I was required to lead some coaching sessions, so I set up a "home office" in our living room. At the same time, I started to apply these coaching skills in my own life and got the crazy notion that maybe these skills could assist others interested in living a more authentic life. So, I went to Home Depot to buy a small desk and set up a telephone and Macintosh computer in the living room.

But working from home with two children had its challenges. On good days I could use my imagination to put healthy parent/child boundaries in place. I put a few small toys in a special cardboard box in our dining area, about 15 feet from my desk. The corner with the telephone and computer became both our family living space and my office. So, in order for it to "convert" into my office, we set up an agreement. When I was on the phone, the boys could open the cardboard box in the dining room. When the phone calls were done, the box was closed and off limits until the next one. I put a lot of effort into this darn box, only to discover later that the art and science of making forts was way more interesting. Eventually, I eliminated the special box, and understood the total awe of boxes, blankets, and duct tape.

One of the tools that I learned during my coach training was called the Life Wheel. I later adapted the Life Wheel to become my number-one go-to tool as an executive coach in the workplace. The roots of it however, originated at the kitchen table of our small dining room.

Here is how the Life Wheel works.

Taylor, at age five, would draw a circle and divide it into eight wedges. Then we would label these wedges with the things that support a well-balanced life. As a young family, we named the wedges like this:

1. School

2. Allowance

3. Friends/Family

4. Health: Our bodies and mind

5. Passion

6. Spirit/Prayer/Church

7. Fun & Play

8. Home

Then we could each rate our individual wedges on a scale of 1–10, with 1 feeling low and 10 feeling great. This was a good way to organize a conversation about what was happening to us, especially given all of the transitions we were experiencing.

I would pull out the blank Life Wheels as a way to connect when I felt things were going particularly well, so I could listen for how Taylor and I would describe things in our own words. We could focus on what was going right, figure it out, and then put our attention on doing more of that, whatever "that" was. I would also pull out blank paper to draw our wheels when something felt hard or bad or heavy, so I could listen for how we might describe those moments. Given that Jonathan and I shared 50/50 custody, I wanted to stay attuned to their experience of their whole lives, not just a section of it.

One day when I thought things we going particularly well, I pulled out some blank paper at the kitchen table. Taylor and I drew our wheels. Zachary hung out beside me. Taylor completed his wheel first, and it took my breath away.

He had rated his "friends" category at a 2. Up until this moment, I thought this was one of our strong suits. Given that we lived walking distance to the elementary school they both attended, I thought this wedge would be a no-brainer because he could visit the playground about any time he wanted.

"Tell us how the friend category got a 2," I asked.

"I like my friends," Taylor said. "It's just that whenever I invite them over, you tell me to tell them not to come over because Zachary is having seizures."

"Oh... yeah."

Later that day I called a counselor in tears. I didn't want Taylor to feel ashamed or embarrassed in front of his friends who didn't have experience with seizures. I also knew that I had masterfully covered this up. I would make sure that people didn't make fun of Taylor's brother, so I protected him, at the expense of Taylor's growing social awareness.

I didn't know what Taylor knew.

I didn't know that he was naturally creative, resourceful, and whole. I didn't know that at even a young age, Zachary and Taylor were finding their way to be fully themselves, and keeping commitments and playing with friends was an important part of finding their way.

My counselor recommended I develop a structure, like ordering pizza for an after-school snack once a week when Taylor wanted to invite a friend over. The pizza would be my reminder that no matter how intense Zachary's seizures were on that day, we would find our way and it was important for Taylor's friends to still come over and play. I needed to relearn how to keep our word to each other.

Being a single mom of two young children, one with severe disabilities, was one thing.

Listening to my non-stop inner dialogue of what a good mom should be was another.

It was relentless: How can I feel bored and overwhelmed in my life at the same time? How come I hurry the boys' bedtime routine and even skip reading at night? Is something wrong with me?

One morning as we were getting ready, David and his daughter drove by and screamed out the window "Hey, Zachary!" on their way to Shepardson Elementary. This made me feel almost normal, part of the community. As we ate our cereal, I asked Taylor, "Well, as you rotate between two homes and go to school, what kinds of things are you noticing?"

He paused, then said, "Boys and girls are really different from each other."

"I noticed that, too. How would you describe the different things?"

"Easy. Boys like to watch sports and girls just like to be with boys so that is why they watch sports. Girls need a lot of choices for clothes to wear, and boys just want a pair of jeans and a shirt. Boys like to fart and burp and make loud noises with their bodies. Girls think it's disgusting."

Like other kids his age, Taylor had a childlike way of simply noticing the world around him without putting judgments on his observations. I was relearning this childlike skill of simply noticing myself. I was noticing new ways to see the world. I was noticing new ways to see each other. I was noticing the power of listening.

The more I could let go of trying to be a single mom the "right" way and listen to my kids and the metaphors around us, the more I could find our path to live our life. As I opened up to these moments of listening to the world more deeply, I still felt a paradox in my gut. I kept trying to map out a plan for our life, yet the moments that brought secret joy were the moments of gathering clues from our environment. It was almost as if things like the song on the radio, the change in the weather, and the newspaper headlines on the dining table provided clues on this scavenger hunt to create our life.

Standing in the garage, looking for gasoline and not feeling in the mood to do yard work, I heard Savage Garden sing:

"I am counting on a new beginning

A reason for living

A deeper meaning—yeah…"

So, I found the gasoline, asked Taylor if he wanted to mow or weed wack, and we did yard work. Just by listening to those words, I let go of exhaustion and grabbed a little energy to work together.

I continued to build my own muscle of connecting with Zachary. I discovered that when I faced him heart-to-heart with eye contact, I felt a sense of deep intimacy quickly. Unlike other relationships that were filled with clarifying questions, interruptions, and misunderstandings, communicating with Zachary felt simple. Still, when people asked me really thoughtful questions like "How do you communicate with Zachary?" or "How should I communicate with Zachary?" sometimes the best answer I could muster up was something like "I dunno."

The only thing that stopped me was that I didn't want Zachary to be a victim of my attitude problem. So I went on a search to hire a professional Zachary whisperer, someone who had credentials, so I could purchase an hour of their time, get a certified explanation about how to officially communicate with my son. I was introduced to a woman, Sharissa Joy, who impacted me for life.

Sharissa was a consultant, trainer, author, and editor. She was earning her degree in Psychology/Sociology with honors from Denver University. I had heard her presentation about her own experience of living with disabilities years before, and her personal stories rocked my world. Sharissa used PowerPoint and a facilitative communication device as a presenter. I had never listened to someone who did not speak tell their life story with such potent messages and haunting images.

On the day she came to Fort Collins, she and her dad, who was also her care provider, arrived in the late morning. I wanted to make the best use of our 60 minutes together, so I had gone through my own dress rehearsal the week before. I told her Zachary's history, explained what I loved about him, and told her how exhausting it was for me to try to teach people how to communicate with him. I showed her how I communicated with him, and then I had Taylor tell her some things that he knew about Zachary.

Sharissa used a facilitative communication (FC) device. Her father explained the FC is a technique used by some caregivers and educators to assist people with severe disabilities communicate more effectively. It works when there is a special bond between a person with a disability and their caregiver. The person with the severe disability points to letters on an alphabet keyboard; the facilitator gently holds the other person's hand or arm to guide it, sometimes providing additional emotional or moral support. I remembered hearing lots of controversy from people about how this worked. It seemed like some people were skeptical that the person facilitating the hand of the other person could manipulate the situation to convey a message they wanted to share. Either way, I had heard Sharissa Joy speak when a computer was hooked up to her FC device and her message felt profoundly clear and real to me. I had no doubts in Sharissa's approach to communicate. I wondered if Zachary's arm would ever loosen up enough that we could do this someday.

As she got to work, I watched the intensity on Sharissa's face. She avoided eye contact, ignored personal space boundaries, and was extremely focused on Zachary. I felt awkward trying to organize our time together, but I desperately wanted her advice. The most important thing was that I wanted her to spend time with Zachary, since both of them were nonverbal, and then tell me what I could tell the rest of the world about how to connect with him.

After she spent some time sitting with Zachary, it was time for Sharissa to provide me with recommendations. She was authoritative. Her message was clear. Sharissa used her facilitative communication device to say: "Shut Up. It is exhausting to live in a yakety-yaker's world."

That was it.

That was her entire recommendation, and then she and her dad left.

I felt like the wind had been knocked out of me—at once disappointed by this recommendation while at the same time ashamed, as in I should have organized our time a bit differently so that I could have leveraged her expertise in a better way. Somewhere in the back of my mind, I was horrified she had told me something it would take years for me to actually hear.

In the upcoming months, I used an egg timer in our small living room and an hourglass timer in the kitchen. I would sit down so that I was slightly lower than Zachary and face him heart to heart. I would make eye contact and not speak until all the sand filled the bottom of the hourglass. It was an incredibly dynamic process. It usually started with me feeling a bit fake, fidgety, or uncomfortable. Then, in no linear progression, I would experience a combination of sad thoughts, weird thoughts, grocery-list thoughts, how-much-more-time thoughts, healing thoughts, kind thoughts, loving thoughts. I kept using the timer, the same way I would buy pizza when Taylor had a friend come over: both were structures that reminded me of my focus.

When I was at ease with myself and allowed myself to "not know" how to communicate with Zachary, something borderline mysterious would happen. It was almost like when I (an extrovert) would have random moments of cultivating my own inner silence, and then something shifted in my communication with Zachary. Something happened in that moment—a union between Zachary and me. I didn't know it at the time, though, eventually, I realized that in order for me to cultivate a relationship with someone who is non-verbal, I needed to begin cultivating my own inner silence. Then and only then could I be present enough to actually develop a deep and personal relationship with Zachary.

It took years for me to build my own way of knowing that communication with Zachary was more about intention over technique. In other words, just like a good meditation practice, communicating with Zachary started with not judging myself. It was a chance to let go of multi-tasking and simply be present with another soul. The irony was that my ability to communicate with Zachary was more about a gentle and loving process to learn how to spend time with *myself*. In so many of my other verbal relationships, I had conditioned myself so I could go through the motions of relationships easily. I could toss on any mask I wanted in the moment and surf through a conversation easily enough. Communicating with someone beyond the words, however, was a very different experience. I learned in raising Zachary much more about my ability to actually listen, experience the grace of one another, and allow moments of deep intimacy through silence and true connection.

Eventually, I became more comfortable in describing how others could communicate with Zachary. I passed along my own experience of what Sharissa Joy taught me. I suggested:

- Sitting at eye level

- Breathing and connecting with self first

- Beginning each conversation with "not knowing" what our conversation would be about

- Cultivating a relationship with the unknown

- Noticing how the body, mind, spirit are connected and get moving if energy was low

- Speak authentically, and then listen and repeat

This makes so much sense now, though at the time, I was having very parallel experiences. I noticed that sometimes when I was hanging with Zachary, my head was spinning with thoughts, and I acted like I was not multi-tasking, though I was. There were days it was just inevitable and probably normal that I was near him and not remotely paying attention to him.

My training as a coach offered three distinctions: Put attention on other person, be future focused, and believe the other person was naturally creative, resourceful, and whole. This, combined with my experience of connecting Zachary to the yakety-yaker's world, was all related. It's just that sometimes I couldn't discern when I was part of the solution and when I was getting in my own way.

The silver lining of my near-constant feelings of inadequacy was that there were no role models to follow. No rules made sense to me. So, the tendency I had in life to test the limits, ignore my mistakes, and seek variety in our daily routines would sometimes work to strengthen our family.

As Michelle partnered with Zachary to unpack some boxes one summer day, I grabbed Taylor to go find a few cans of cheap paint. I had an idea, though I didn't exactly have a plan. Taylor and I drove down the road to Builder's Square hardware store. We walked across the parking lot, got a shopping cart, and headed for the paint aisle. We stopped at the brightly lit area filled with strips of paint color. "Taylor, what color paint would you like to get?" I knew that one way I could ensure my kids had a few memories of something going right was giving them the power to make decisions.

Taylor grabbed a fist of bright-colored paint strips. "The rainbow color."

I walked down the aisle to find the smallest cans of orange, red, blue and green paint. On our way home, I imagined what we could do with the paint. It was a warm weekend afternoon, so I took both boys to our little garage. I opened the cans, along with some other leftover Crayola powder paints and laid out some plastic by the north and west walls. The three garage walls were completely blank—a perfect canvas. I had a little talk with myself to let them paint whatever portions of the garage walls they wanted, and then I could embellish and add to the top portion. After all, our garage door was often open, and I didn't want neighbors to think I was an unruly neighbor.

So, the directions were simple and clear. They could paint any area they wanted.

I left to go get some water, and when I came back, I was more than surprised. I was struck by the complete miscommunication we had.

Zachary was sitting in his floor-level scooter, all strapped in. Taylor had plopped down in front of him and proceeded to use the 2" paintbrush to cover Zachary's body in orange and red. I didn't say anything, and neither did they. As Taylor finished painting Zachary, he just kept going and painted himself. He painted himself blue and red and orange, which eventually turned into a mud color. I put my attention on painting the west wall. Later that afternoon, the three of us painted the north wall of the garage. Many years later, when Zachary was twenty-three and moved back into 1808 Centennial Road, the garage walls remained the bright hues of their childhood.

Michelle had many superpowers. One was picking up on our need to create a kind of daring and fun spirit in our home. Knowing that I was a bit creative, open-minded, and impatient with details, she asked if she and Zachary could paint the boys' bedroom. She put Zachary to work by having him hold paintbrushes while she talked about the colors. Eventually our little condo was fully painted, and the only things left white were the sinks and toilets installed by the previous owners.

I started to "notice," or as I learned in my coach training, "simply notice" all the narrators in my head. I would discern the screaming inner critic that wanted me to accept all the pre-conceived notions about what a good mom or bad mom would do. It was only in those rare moments of painting the garage walls together or other creative endeavors that I could briefly let go of all of the medications, seizure documentation, medical appointments, broken equipment, and checklist of things from last month I hadn't done. I could stop the screaming voice of how disappointed my ex-husband was in me and actually feel OK about feeling OK.

Eventually, I was able to build the muscle to recognize that I could normalize moments of pleasure within myself regardless of our circumstances, rather than try to control the circumstances. The times I could do this tended to be when it was sunny and there were no expectations, or complete darkness and I was too exhausted to fight with myself.

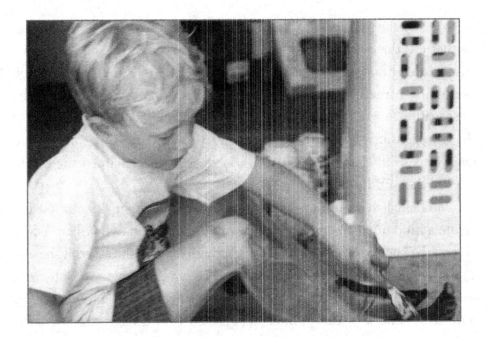

CHAPTER 6

REINVENTING MYSELF THROUGH COACHING

As I trained to become a coach, I spent a lot of time reflecting. I would grab 10 minutes in the parking lot, five minutes while pureeing Zachary's food, and random moments on the toilet trying to complete the books required for my training. I was like a sponge soaking up new perspectives. The storm that was brewing inside of me was trying to find a way to internalize these radical new life lessons.

On the one hand, I was experiencing a sense of mindfulness and connectedness when I could be still with Zachary, like Sharissa Joy had taught me, though this feeling lasted for only a blink before I was tangled in the noise of the world around me.

I had learned the skills of coaching presence or "being present" through my training. We got feedback in our ability to be present and flexible during conversations, like dancing in the moment. Master coaches observed our ability to access our own intuition, trust our inner knowing, and "go with our gut" as needed. We were taught to see many ways to listen to others and choose in the moment the most effective way to lead the conversation.

Ultimately, we were trained to confidently shift people's perspectives so that our clients could experiment with new possibilities and new actions. I was working as fast as I could to integrate this skill into my core sense of self. I tried noticing when I could stay present in the moment versus when I would get overpowered with fear. I needed to practice this skill in my own life before I could become good at doing this with others.

I started doing yoga in my living room. I cut pictures out of a magazine—images of waterfalls, hiking trails, and trees—and taped them on a piece of poster board. On random mornings I would light a candle, turn on soft music, get on the mat, and attempt to be inspired by my nature collage. My typical yoga practice lasted 90 seconds, though I told myself at least I got on the mat.

It felt like I was gaining knowledge, experience, and training for a reason, but I couldn't put my finger on it. I was slowly rediscovering a little bit of my creativity, living a bit more in the moment rather than being consumed with fear about living near poverty with my children, and maybe even getting in touch with my purpose in life. I felt hope for Zachary, Taylor, myself, and others who didn't quite have a roadmap for life, yet I wasn't sure how to apply these new tools in our single-parent family or on a broader scale.

In preparation for the CICC meetings, Barbara Stutsman and I would meet Elizabeth Hepp for lunch while the boys were in school. As we sat in a local Mexican restaurant, I would take risks. I began to find comfort in telling Elizabeth things I found difficult to admit to myself. I told her that I didn't know if I was the kind of person who could raise Zachary. I didn't know anything about disabilities, and I wanted to ignore the entire disability industry. I felt depressed whenever I thought about visiting a place restricted to educating or housing people with disabilities. There were so many broken assumptions about people, and I feared that I would start to feel more broken or less broken than people with disabilities, and either way, it put a knot in my stomach. I was more comfortable being in places where we came together as people first and then found ways to get real in creating meaningful lives for each other, one conversation at a time. Elizabeth could walk in this thick cloud surrounding me and be with me and not get lost.

"I'm worried about how Zachary is fitting into his Kindergarten class," I told her as we were wrapping up our afternoon meeting.

"Yeah, most parents are." Elizabeth motioned for the waiter to bring the check. "It's important to stay focused on the important stuff like circle time, eating snacks, and playing outside together."

"Well, I was thinking about kids staring at him and feeling awkward and avoiding him, so then he will be lonely, and then I'm supposed to feel like I don't notice."

"Exactly—that's what most parents worry about. You'll get to be part of a series of conversations so that you can work with his teacher and support team to creatively brainstorm what cushions best support him on the floor at circle time, the best snacks for him to eat, how to assist him to eat, and the kinds of adaptive equipment the school may have on the playground. The best part is that you and the team can create a vision of possibilities for Zachary, and the team will collaborate with each other to make it happen. In fact, go ahead and ask his team to engage the kids to come up with ideas, too. That's all part of the early-childhood-education approach."

I looked at her in disbelief. "Why would they be willing to do that? I don't remember other families including their children with severe disabilities in the classroom."

"It is all related to the civil rights movement and the implementation of recent public policy that says all children belong in 'natural environments.' The law now states that all the resources that used to pay for kids to be segregated are now required to make a sharp left turn and spend those same dollars in a different way. Rather than building separate schools, separate pools, separate clubs and activities, professionals are required to find new ways to build inclusive communities."

"That sounds good for other kids. Zachary is just not going to fit in."

"Zachary is going to thrive. How else can I support you?"

"I have no idea. I do feel a little more hopeful right now, though..."

Susan, too, was a guide who could help me and other young parent leaders navigate the wilderness of childhood inclusion. She knew both the spirit and legal aspects of the new public policies and laws. She quietly spoke with deep conviction of what was possible even when I expressed my deepest fears: "I am scared to death that these new policies are bogus. I cannot imagine how someone like Zachary could actually be included in our neighborhood junior high school with typical peers. How do I walk the talk if I don't believe it can really happen?"

"It can happen," Susan said. "You don't have to do any of this alone. This is the exact purpose of the CICC: to work with systems across Colorado to re-invent how the current public dollars can be used in new ways to support kids like Zachary. It is possible. It is also the right thing to do."

One by one, these people walked beside me with my fears, concerns, and often clunky and fragmented ideas.

In 1998 I finished my training at the Coaches Training Institute, and by 1999, I took the exam and was certified as a Professional Coach. The Colorado Department of Education (CDE) posted a Request for Proposal (RFP) which included one full-time position. This person would design, develop, and implement a strategy to use coaching skills to develop parent leaders related to IDEA Part C legislation requirements. Barbara was the executive director of the DisAbility Connection, so as part of her role, she took the lead in writing the proposal, which designated me for the position. Barbara was very experienced in managing the administration and financial aspects of grants. During our morning walks, when the boys were staying at their dad's house, she would ask me questions that would inspire me to actually think about what I would want out of this position.

"What is your vision of a future where parents could use coaching skills with their families?"

I thought about this for a moment, and then with a conviction I didn't knew I had, the words tumbled out: "I think about families putting their attention on what is possible and then working with professionals to use current resources to make THAT happen, rather than the old-school way of isolating kids with disabilities in a segregated place somewhere."

"Why is this important to children, family, or providers?"

"Just imagine a world where all children could do the same stuff: go to library hour, sign up for swimming classes, be in the Christmas pageant, get invited to friends' birthday parties, etc. It could be a world where parents would connect as parents *first* by hanging out together rather than feeling isolated, lonely, and broken, without a sense of belonging. And here is the real kicker: imagine physical therapists, social workers, and medical staff who could bring all of themselves to these kinds of conversations—not just the part of them trained to be an expert. People could literally come together and co-create new thoughts, new ideas, and new ways of living meaningful lives. Together we could talk about how to adapt our natural environments to be more inclusive. Imagine an occupational therapist, mom, and child with a disability meeting outside, picking dandelions in the park to gain more finger coordination, rather than in the basement of a hospital."

For weeks she asked and I answered, and a vision of what was possible began to emerge. Barbara then took these conversations and formatted them into a formal request for proposal "RFP." When the CDE reviewed the proposal and awarded us the funding, I was on top of the world. It seemed to me that Barbara must have had a magic wand to connect the dots between what I, a scared single mom, was giving voice to and a big bureaucratic system that was willing to support my vision.

The one-year contract was called "The Coaching Project" and would run from July 1998 to June 1999. Its purpose was to support and enhance parent leadership in families of children with disabilities from birth to three years old with disabilities throughout Colorado. The project focused on a model that introduced eleven coaching competencies to parents interested in developing their own unique leadership skills. It supported the development of leadership skills for parents to promote inclusive communities and provide supports and services in everyday routines, activities, and places.

From CDE's perspective, it was an innovative approach to implement public policy. For me, it was as if those conversations in the last few years were erupting into a volcano of hope. I felt like I was straddling the Grand Canyon. The vision of what was possible was spectacular. I felt a flash of awe as I looked around at the landscape; we would have an opportunity to bring together the old culture of disability with the new peaks and perspectives available through a coaching mindset.

I could feel the possibilities, though I had precious little extra energy, and I, of course, didn't even know what I didn't know. I was also worried about acting like a non-mother in the workplace. It seemed like everyone I knew had a separate identity within his or her career. My identity was still a stay-at-home, frazzled mom trying to keep up with scheduling medical appointments, refilling medications, looking for stamps to pay my bills, and rewriting my to-do list because I couldn't find the last one I wrote.

Thankfully, Barbara would co-lead The Coaching Project. She showed me how the CDE, ECI, and CICC were different teams, councils, and initiatives working together. She mentored me in understanding how the people working among these systems had developed some overall guiding principles that influenced all components of the Part C legislation. One of these principles was the necessary involvement and empowerment of families of children with disabilities. In other words, the leaders serving on the CDE, ECI, and CICC were invested in strategically empowering families in new and innovative ways.

The Coaching Project linked the mission, vision, and values of the CDE with the possibility of implementing Part C legislation in Colorado with fresh eyes. Elizabeth and Susan were on the balcony with Barbara looking across the vast ballroom of what was now possible from a state department perspective. I was on the dance floor, looking up at them and taking cues about how to begin a whole new dance.

Together, we had a year of growth and dynamic collaboration that laid the foundation for The Coaching Project. I worked full-time and especially long hours when the boys were with their dad. We were breaking new ground in discovering ways to introduce a coaching mindset into the lives of families of children with disabilities. The Coaching Project gave me a practical way to start applying what I was learning in my own coach training. Ultimately, I was learning about how a really good leadership coach or business coach had to understand the principle of "calling forth." "Calling forth" in the coaching industry starts with asking questions like "Who are you becoming?" It was based on the awareness that we need to cultivate our own sense of who we are on the inside, and then and only then can we bridge **that** internal awareness with how we want to show up and impact others.

So, the opportunity to direct The Coaching Project allowed me the chance to practice reinventing myself from the inside out and begin to give back in some tiny, small way. Julie had introduced me to the phrase "God wink." I didn't know exactly what it meant, yet I knew exactly how it felt. The opportunity to direct The Coaching Project and develop new structures to introduce shifts in the way we met, planned, and designed our lives (as families of children with disabilities) was a total God wink for me.

Our weekly Monday-morning calls were modeled from the coaching supervision I went through in my certification program, which focused on reflection, exploration, discussion, and professional growth. It was an intimate setting designed to assist each of us in noticing what supported us to be good coaches and get curious about what was blocking us.

In The Coaching Project, I and the five coaches, who were also parents of children with disabilities, conducted these calls as a group. It was as if we were part of a new tribe coming together and developing new kinds of awareness in this sacred group setting. All supervision calls were based on the three coaching tenets: 1. Focus on the other person's agenda, 2. Be future focused, 3. Believe the other person is naturally creative, resourceful, and whole. No advice. The meetings were all by telephone; we used the directions in the front of the Yellow Pages to set up an old-fashioned conference call, where the first person called the second person; then the second person called the third person, and the third person called the fourth person, until we could hear each other. We each discussed one thing that was currently working well in our small-group coaching, one thing we were struggling with, and one resource we thought others in the group could benefit from.

As each parent/coach shared a challenge they were having, I would ask questions, on occasion articulate what I heard going on, and then check it out to see if that was true for the parent/coach. Lucy, one of the five parent coaches, was the mother of a child with a disability who lived on the western slope of Colorado about six hours to the west. She voiced her concern during one of these calls. "One of the moms on our coaching call who is bilingual in Spanish/English was upset with the time she is supposed to take her daughter to physical therapy. It is in the middle of the afternoon, when her other daughter naps."

"That does sound frustrating," I said. "How did you approach the situation?"

"I asked her what the ideal situation would be for her family and if she'd talked about that with the physical therapist."

"What was the mom's response?"

"She said that she had not thought about an ideal situation and felt uncomfortable talking about it with the physical therapist. She was afraid it would be disrespectful."

"How did you coach her at that point?"

"I asked her to take a moment and describe an ideal situation. The mom paused and then said that she could probably keep the same time, though she would just get there earlier so that she could set up a quiet place for her other daughter to take a nap. The appointment is at a small rural clinic with lots of quiet places."

"What did you discover about yourself as a coach in that moment?"

"Well, now that I'm thinking through it, maybe I didn't fail as badly as I thought. I was feeling really bad and felt like I should have come up with advice for her. I am so used to thinking that the only way I can help is to give advice, and maybe her own new idea will work for her."

"How can we support you now?"

"I am looking forward to the next call with this mom to find out what she tried and how it worked for her. Even if the new idea isn't working, I'm feeling a little more confident that we can brainstorm some more options."

"It sounds like you were focused on her agenda, you were also future focused, and you believed she was naturally, creative, resourceful, and whole. It sounds like you were curious and standing beside her shoulder to shoulder and exploring the possibilities together. Nicely done! Thank you for sharing a real-life example of how we can partner in new ways as parents. We'll look forward to connecting next week to see what else you are discovering about yourself as you and we keep building these new muscles."

As coaches, our training had taught us to identify paying clients, though our weekly calls helped us shift from "selling" our coaching service/ "proving" our coaching skills into being more inventive and ingenious with parents. We became more curious about what parents wanted in their lives, and found clarity in how we could add value to the parents' life—just for the joy of it! As new coaches, we learned the power of being unattached to outcomes. We practiced being curious and listening to each other more fully. We started to "do" less coaching and be in more authentic conversations with each other. We were individually and collectively rediscovering our own personal definitions of success.

I continued to feel divided. I worked from my living room 60–70 hours a week when the boys were with Jonathan and 20–25 hours when the boys were with me. Jonathan was distant, and it was clear that he did not have any interest in coach training or my struggle to find a career path. In fact, when I went to his house to pick up the boys, he would not come to the door. I would ring the doorbell, the door would mysteriously open, and Taylor would push Zachary and his wheelchair outside. When Jonathan came to pick up the boys, he would ring our doorbell; then without any eye contact or speaking a single syllable, he would push Zachary down the ramp and walk the boys to the car. The transitions felt cold and semiarid, like the high-desert Colorado mountains. The only communication we had was on the telephone regarding scheduling and the mistakes I made in packing the boys' things each week. The harder I tried to perfect the checklist of things to pack, the more I felt like a failure.

This experience with Jonathan highlighted my appreciation for the space to share thoughts in a safe way with other people. As the other coaches trusted their gut and shared new insights, I scribbled them down: "Enrolling people in a coaching conversation is about getting real about starting a relationship together." "I'm glad I completed my coach training. I did all the learning I could do, though when it comes to interacting with other parents, I seem to throw it all out and just get real." "Each time I try to do a coaching technique I feel like a fraud—it's harder than I thought to just be authentic with others when I'm having such a rough time managing my own life." I was attracted to their humility and realized I was feeling the same things. As other people described their experiences, I could feel my breath getting smoother. My heart grew warm. I could feel something inside of me soften. I felt another layer of my loneliness melt away.

While I was slowly carving a career path with my coaching skills, I practiced the skill of asking the boys "powerful questions." "Powerful questions" we defined as beginning with the word "what" or "how" and have seven or fewer words. The results were often surprising.

"What would be a good family date night?" I asked Taylor on the way home from school one afternoon.

He didn't miss a beat: "I think we should have a food fight for dinner in the backyard on Saturday."

"How would it work?"

"We walk to the grocery store and buy ba-sketti-y, then come home to cook it and then go to the backyard and throw it at each other. Whoever catches it can eat it. Then the rest just gets mowed up the next time you make me mow the lawn."

At the same time, I was trying to put some better boundaries in place for when I was working in the living room and the boys were home from school. I had repeatedly asked them to entertain themselves, and it wasn't working. I didn't even know exactly what I meant by this; I just needed moments of uninterrupted time.

I talked to Zachary and Taylor the same way and figured that they would need to create some of their own adaptations. As young boys I knew that, given the same situation, they would come up with solutions different from me, and I needed them to tap into their own capacity. Finally, I asked Taylor, "What do you want to call the 30 minutes when you need to entertain yourself?"

"I dunno."

"If you did know, what should we call it?"

"Ready to Rumble."

"Okay, so our new code word will be 'Ready to Rumble,' and that means you have 30 minutes to take care of yourself. Does that sound right?"

"Yup."

Zachary listened and watched Taylor like a hawk.

As the Director of The Coaching Project, it was my responsibility to collect data about the outcomes parents experienced as a result of being coached. Some of the common themes I heard ranged from increased confidence in self, being curious and engaged in creative problem solving related to their child's typical day, and noticing different perspectives about how to live a meaningful life. Families felt comfortable being more actively engaged in the decision process with pediatricians, neurologists, physical therapists, and all the other specialists that rotated through their lives. The coaching experience also inspired them to dream big while being unattached to the outcomes. Families expressed more courage to play with dish soap, make bubbles, and add food coloring to leftover spaghetti to make spaghetti potion. Some mothers and fathers even began asking challenging questions of case managers and social workers by taking a stand on an issue, rather than automatically agreeing with professionals and silently signing documents. One father really wanted to know if his daughter could attend an in-home day care/preschool, and after a series of discussions, they found the perfect match.

One challenge we soon discovered is that the parents of young children with disabilities who completed individual coaching sessions acknowledged that, when they reached out to other parents of children with disabilities, there was a big disconnect. Many parents of children with disabilities had not had the support to imagine new possibilities with their child/families. As a result, a recommendation was made for the next year's Coaching Project to focus on strengthening the link between The Coaching Project and various other projects funded by the CDE.

Interestingly, some parents reported that coaching calls seemed strange and too personal. I, too, had my own experience of resisting the idea of sharing my feelings with people, though in my coach training I had begun to feel safe to hone my story and share my experience in baby steps.

In follow-up telephone surveys, some parents requested that coaching calls be redesigned and focus on how they could help others, rather than talk about themselves. So much of their private lives was talked about in frequent medical appointments that they wanted something that felt less invasive. The next coaching project would discuss ways to link the coaching concepts in less-intimidating ways, thus allowing parents to actually re-connect with their feelings of being naturally creative, resourceful, and whole.

Another hope for The Coaching Project was to provide a method to offer a similar coaching experience on a larger scale. So, during that first year, we designed a series of workshops for people to learn and experience some of the coaching skills Barbara and I and the five other parents had learned in our coach training. We conducted 18 workshops in local communities across Colorado and impacted 217 people (parenting a child from birth to age three with a disability). Participants included birth mothers, birth fathers, adoptive mothers, adoptive fathers, teenage mothers, grandparents, siblings, monolingual Spanish-speaking parents, bilingual parents, and foster parents, parents with disabilities, and parents with paid roles working with Part C local agencies.

We designed the curriculum, developed participant packets, and coordinated logistics to effectively reach out across key geographical areas in Colorado. One of the local agency providers saw me doodling and sketching children. She encouraged me to add my sketches to the header of the packets. I felt embarrassed, as well as flattered. Soon I was adding cartoon-like drawings of children in wheelchairs playing outdoors, kids of all abilities on the playground, children of different ethnic backgrounds sitting in the sandbox, and toddlers hanging from rocks or running through water hoses.

Barbara encouraged me to hand out evaluations so that we could gather parents' insights from workshop participants. Families experienced moments of energy. They reported feeling like they had more choices in life and more confidence to ask questions. They had strategies to "chunk down" tasks that overwhelmed them and took baby steps to get things done. Parents expressed a feeling of hope and courage to take more risks rather than waiting until everything was just right. One mom wrote about her first realization that it was okay to focus on her own well-being so that she would be less angry in taking care of her family. One small group of parents acknowledged that each time they had been saying "yes" to something, they were unconsciously saying "no" to something else.

I drove more than 300 miles to Grand Junction alone in May to lead a workshop. The drive was relaxing and fed the adventure part of my soul. I found myself excited by the views along I-70 of the canyons, mesas, and biking trails of Summit County. I drove through the vineyards of the western slope where local wineries made chardonnay and merlot. I had packed only two long-sleeved blouses and forgot how chilly it was when I got gas in Leadville, the highest city in the United States, nicknamed the "Two-Mile-High City," with an altitude of 10,151 feet above sea level.

The interstate also passed through the ski resort of Vail and the natural hot springs of Glenwood Springs. I felt transported into the beauty of nature and the exotic sense of not needing to think about medical stuff. I was nervous, however, that I was going alone without a lifeline to anyone from CDE, the CICC, or any other agency. Usually there was another person who had my back in the audience of the other workshops. This one was going to be led by just me, by myself, outside of my comfort zone.

I still did not know the disability industry, and I didn't want to know much about it. I didn't know much about different diagnoses, local agencies, or anything outside the coaching books I had been reading. The workshop took place in a sterile municipal building. My mouth felt dry no matter how much water I drank. There were 110 people in the room, and the front rows were empty. A few people sat in the middle rows, and the rest of the folks stood in the back with their arms crossed. I tried to smile and walk up to the people in the middle rows to introduce myself, though it was obvious that I was the stranger in the room. As the workshop began, a tall gentleman with a straw-colored cowboy hat raised his hand. "Mam, we have a certain way of doin' things over here. So there ain't no need to drive all the way over here and confuse us with the facts." I was uncomfortable the rest of the afternoon, though another family from this workshop later shared, "Now I understand there are different perspectives; nothing is black and white. I can look for colors, give voice to my own perspective, and learn from others rather than being defensive or scared."

The more I coached people, the more I realized I was not alone in my experience of raising Zachary. I noticed how this journey of raising a child with a disability was uncharted territory for all of us. Parents who participated in group-coaching conversations across the state talked about the complexities of their new life. I was able to speak more openly about my own nightmares, hopes, and dreams. I was struck by how much I had in common with others who at first glance looked so different from me. I had similar fears as a dad in a rural community outside Pueblo. I had similar hopes to a mom who was an attorney in Durango, and newly hatching dreams like a Spanish-speaking mom in Summit County. As a coach and a mom, I experienced a repeated ability to create safe and supportive environments. It was in those environments that we quietly championed each other to consider new thoughts, new ideas, and new beliefs about our families. Even if it invoked a fear of failure or thinking about sensitive new areas, we began to trust ourselves in new ways. We could begin to let go of this notion that we were not good enough.

With my newfound (though at times still shaky) confidence, I didn't compare myself as often with neighbors who had fancy outdoor Little Tike playground sets or video games and electronics. Instead, I found a 36" × 48" world map at the used bookstore and attached it to a wall in our dining room/kitchen. Each country was labeled. I also found place mats with a map where each country was outlined, though not named. We created a memory game that became part of our morning routine. I would ask Taylor to choose any country he wanted from the giant map on the

wall. He would say it and tell us something about where it was on the map. The next day he would tell us the country from the day before and then choose a new country. He would tell us something about where the new country was on the map. This became a cumulative activity until he got up to nearly 45 countries that he could recite by looking at the paper placemats with outlines of each country.

Sometimes I just didn't know how to spend time together as a fragile single-parent family, so putting our attention on something was better than nothing. We found ways to establish our own routines, and I slowly found ways to create boundaries without feeling like a mean mom.

By the end of the first year of The Coaching Project, I felt something wake up inside of me that I did not even know was asleep. We applied for funding for the next year with a new tag line: "An Innovative Approach Supporting Leaders to: Accelerate the Achievement of Organizational Outcomes and Personal Definitions of Success!"

The quote that I posted on my bathroom mirror was by Patrick Overton. It said: "When we walk to the edge of all the light we have to take the step into the darkness of the unknown, we must believe that one of two things will happen. There will be something solid for us to stand on or we will be taught how to fly."

It was 1999. I was a single mom finding courage to fly.

CHAPTER 7

RISKING LOVE

In the fall, a dear friend of mine generously gifted my friend Mai, Stephanie, and me a place to stay in Costa Rica. Jonathan agreed to keep the boys a few extra days, so we booked our tickets to San Jose, Costa Rica to begin a sort of pilgrimage together. The journey was incredibly intimate for me, in part because I was traveling with two women who knew a bit more about me than I knew myself.

Mai was fully alive and on fire. We had met during the CTI leadership program. I had never met anyone like her before. She was from Ho Chi Minh City, Vietnam, studied at John F. Kennedy University, and spoke with personal convictions that could be intimidating. She could talk strategy, sex, technology, humanity, or anything else. In her world, there were new rules to live by: Stop walking on eggshells and live a life of vitality. Go the edge and jump. Wake up. Today, tonight, and in-between. Live from passion, and don't let friends hide. So, when we were on the bus finding our way to our destination, I wasn't too surprised when Mai suggest that I buy a padded bra.

"Well, in the unlikely event that I ever go on a date and even more unlikely go on a second date or get serious…. You know."

"What?"

"You know, what if they want me to take off my bra. Wouldn't that be a big disappointment?"

"Oh. Hon-ey. A guy get excited to see a womans naked, and once a womans is naked, he is not disappointed by anything." Mai could talk about anything, just not with correct grammar and proper placement of the "s." She tended to place an "s" in words that didn't need it and exclude it when it was needed.

"Hummm… I'm going to have to think about this."

One afternoon we were sitting on a porch under a thatched roof of our hotel. I could hear the roar of the ocean, see lizards darting under rocks, and smell things that belonged in an aromatherapy store. Howling monkeys were visible in the trees. These were among the largest primates in the world and were famous for their loud howls, which could travel three miles through dense rainforest. The owner walked around topless, and the only other people staying with us were three American men who had come to surf. So, the whole vibe of the place was a bit sensual and organic.

Stephanie, with her long red hair and red freckled skin on which she smothered SFP 50 water-resistant sunscreen every few hours, was stretched out in a hammock. Though her eyes were closed, she had a mischievous grin on her face, so it was hard to tell if she was napping or listening.

As we sipped tea, Mai, who had attended all the leadership training sessions at the same time as I, started to ask me if I was ready to date. I nodded, though could not speak.

"Let make a list of whos you want to manifest and attracts in your life."

I burped out, "The only words I know are what I don't want."

"Okay—then I will says word. If you like them, write them on this pieces of paper. If you don't like them, don't write the word downs."

I wrote the list on the back of a scrap of paper:

- Likes me
- Listens so I feel heard

- Is willing to have his life impacted by me
- Is willing to let me be part of his inner world
- Be curious and sensual
- Talks
- Good conversations, travel, explore, and dance
- Smiles
- Practices a sense of spirituality that permeates life
- Touches me and likes to be touched
- Eye contact
- Adventurous and likes to be near water, trees, and living a "wild" life rather than safe life
- Likes visiting Boulder

Writing these words down were baby steps for me in this process. Mai was queen of creating holding environments. She was masterful at seeing who people had been, who people were, and then getting down to business to bridge them into their next best self. I learned so much from Mai as we lived together for those days. She had an agenda to strip off the false mask I had worked so hard to create and then discover about what was authentically trying to emerge next. I still carry that scrap of paper with the list in my wallet today.

As our CTI leadership program completed, we were required to set a BHAG (Big Hairy Audacious Goal) that was extremely outside our comfort zone. Though I was comfortable talking with men in a professional role I had zippo—zero—less than nothing confidence in talking to a guy without a role or a goal or a task to focus on. I had kissed only two guys in my life, one in high school, and Jonathan, so I did not have much experience in this area. So my great big scary goal for the next 12 months was to make eye contact with three men and not run away. I told Julie about it. She respectfully didn't comment. Instead, something else happened. She was attending a seminar at Kodak where her husband, Rick, was doing Black Belt Six Sigma presentation to a large audience. Julie sat between Rick and his friend Meg, a chemical engineer. In between presentations, Meg told Julie to keep an eye on Mike Houdek when he got up to present his Black Belt Six Sigma project. According to Meg, Mike was a good catch. Julie asked some more questions about him and then suggested he and I go on a blind date. Within a month, Mike called me. For better or worse, I was visiting Alamosa, Colorado, doing a Leadership I workshop and forgot to unplug the fax machine in our small living room and re-plug the telephone into my one phone jack.

Since I worked until 5:00PM in Alamosa, I drove to nearby Salida to spend the night. When I awoke, there was four feet of snow in the driveway, and the owner of the local B&B said I would not be driving out of town that day. The boys were scheduled to be at Jonathan's, so I decided to spend the day in the little town. My one adventure was to walk to the Great Wall Chinese restaurant. I ordered hot & sour soup, four eggrolls, and brown rice. When I got the bill, I opened my fortune cookie.

"Expect a significant change in your life."

I wrote the date and location on the back of the fortune. I also wrote the words "in bed" at the end of the fortune, because Mai taught me to always say each time I read a fortune cookie aloud. The voice inside my head said, "Oh yeah—I dare you. Bring him to me, and watch me make some serious eye contact. I dare you, world."

The snow melted, and I drove north to Fort Collins. I made my way up the ramp to the front door, walked in, and dropped everything on the dining table. I noticed Julie had put a business card of Mike's on my refrigerator. I stared at his photo on the card. He looked nice. Actually, he looked really handsome. He had short brown hair, round glasses, broad shoulders and a warm smile invoking a sense of confidence and excitement. He looked athletic, intelligent, and a bit out of my league. I practiced making eye contact with his business card photo. A few days later, I heard that he'd tried calling, though he kept getting a fax machine sound.

I continued to tackle my BHAG of making eye contact with three men, though I was having a rough start. I wasn't exactly sure where to meet men so that I could complete my assignment. I told myself I just needed to get more creative, so I decided to switch banks from US Bank to Key Bank. US Bank was the one I had used when I was married. I choose Key Bank because I noticed they had two male bank tellers, and this was a good-enough criterion for me to both establish a new identity as a single mom and make progress on my BHAG assignment.

Mike called again, and this time the phone rang. I picked it up.

"H-ell-o?"

"Hi—this is Mike Houdek. Julie gave me your number and suggested I call. How are you?"

My mind went completely blank as I searched for something to say. He was obviously comfortable talking to a woman. He was personable and at some point asked if I would be interested in going out on a date.

"Uh…sure."

"Are you available Saturday, May 1st around 6:00PM?"

"Uh…yeah."

David, Julie, and Barbara had given me three recommendations as I started out into the terrifying world of dating: 1. Don't let my kids meet men that I dated until I became serious, 2. Be my true self—don't be nervous, and don't try to be someone else, 3. Stay relaxed and have fun.

So, Barbara took me shopping for a new outfit at the local outlet mall. I bought a Liz Claiborne black-and-white jumper that I could wear with the white blouse I had worn to the bank when I closed on the condo. I bought a new pair of white tights in tall and had a pair of comfortable black rubber soled shoes in my closet. Julie came over an hour early, and Michelle, our beloved care provider, was there to watch the boys.

I was dressed an hour before Mike arrived. Julie poured me a glass of wine. I did not have much drinking experience, in part because people who drank in college intimidated me. And, since Zachary's birth, I didn't dare drink because we were off to the ER at any moment to manage his increasing seizure activity.

After two glasses of wine, I spilled all over my new jumper. I took it off, scrubbed it by hand, then started to dry it with my old blow dryer and finished drying it with my iron. The white tights were okay, though I was falling apart quickly.

The doorbell rang, and Taylor answered the door. I seemed to be already breaking the few rules I was told about dating. Mike wore a tweed sport jacket, white oxford button down-shirt, jeans, and cowboy boots. He was more than six feet tall in his boots, and muscular. He stood there with a bouquet of flowers and an umbrella over his head. It was a rare night, in many ways. We seldom got rain in Fort Collins, let alone in the evenings, but here it was drizzling out, and there he was, standing and waiting to be asked inside. Julie took the flowers that Mike handed me and put them in a vase with water. Mike introduced himself, and we all made small talk. Then Mike burst out with a joke:

"Hey everybody—A skeleton walks into the bar. He walks up to the bartender and orders a beer and a mop!"

He laughed. I didn't even smile.

I quickly kissed the boys good-bye, thanked Michelle and Julie for being there, amd picked up my REI blue Gore-Tex jacket. Mike opened the door and unfastened the umbrella, but I was already gone. He later told me how surprised he was that I'd just bolted for his red Honda in the driveway.

I opened the car door on the passenger's side and jumped in. It had not occurred to me that he was going to walk me to the car and open the door.

We went to a nice place for cocktails, and then to dinner.

Although I did a lot of preparation so that I could go out this one night, I had failed to think about any topics not related to single-parenting, childcare, disabilities, medical appointments, sleepless nights, fears that kept me up at night, etc. I had nothing "normal" to talk about, so I didn't say much.

Mike was an excellent conversationalist talking about his horses, cats, and dogs. He talked about building a barn with hand tools and asked me questions like if I was a morning person and if I was vegetarian or ate meat. I did pretty well at answering his yes/no questions, though I couldn't for the life of me offer any topics of discussion or even talk about myself. I did eventually make eye contact, so I considered the evening a total homerun. I could go back to my BHAG and document another checkmark.

Our second date was a bit more conversational. We ate dinner at a little French restaurant with candlelit ambiance and lace curtains. Mike asked if I liked champagne.

"Probably." I couldn't remember ever having any.

The waiter brought champagne with a splash of Chambord with an appetizer of baked brie cheese and a not-too-sweet sauce. It was followed with a Caesar salad with anchovies. I kept telling myself to smile and nod and imitate all the other grown-ups in the room. Just like the uncharted territory of Zachary's diagnosis when I looked around to get clues from more experienced people, I was doing the same thing. How in the heck do people spend the evening together?

On our third date, Mike surprised me. He asked me to pack a rain jacket and sunglasses, and wear comfortable shoes. We drove to a trail at Lory State Park and hiked to the top of Arthur's Rock. At the top, he opened his backpack and pulled out a quart-sized bag of insulated ice. He unwrapped glass stemware and two crystal champagne glasses. He slowly filled each of the glasses with champagne and offered a toast.

"Here's to spending time outdoors together."

It was May 9, Mother's Day, and occasionally other hikers looked at us and said, "Happy Mother's Day." I just smiled. I couldn't figure out if my life was becoming more divided by establishing a sense of self away from the boys or artificially united by posing like a couple when in fact it was just our third date.

At any rate, I had started to find my words by this point. Actually, the champagne kicked in, and I was bubbling. I started asking him questions. "What are your life dreams?" "What are the top 10 things that feel good to you?" I was surprised by his candor and honesty. Mike and I were 10 years apart in age, and he had been single for 13 years after a two-year marriage. He did not have any kids, though he had dated a lot of women, some who did have children. He was interested in meeting a woman who was adventurous, outdoors-oriented, and comfortable in jeans or an evening gown. He liked living in the country, and he like cultural things like Shakespeare plays, concerts, poetry, art, and horseback camping. He wanted to have a baby (horse) someday to raise from birth, he liked getting cards in the mail, he liked going to Boulder to watch the CU football games, and he wanted to get good at tango dancing.

It was after this that I went home and hand-wrote a five-page, single-spaced, double-sided letter about how though I might be in a 35-year-old woman's body, I was not experienced with dating, or even confident in the whole realm of intimacy. If he was invested in an open and honest relationship, though, I was going to put all of my fears and concerns on paper and mail it to him.

I addressed the envelope and put a stamp on it.

Mike got the letter, though I wasn't sure when, and I was starting to regret ever sending it. A couple days later, he stopped by our house. He left his home in Bellvue at 4:30AM each day, so when he stopped by at 5:00AM, the boys were still in bed.

"I got your letter," he said, hanging up his coat. "Thank you for writing all of that. There is no need to be nervous. One of the things I think is really important in a healthy relationship is to put a focus on the "you," the "me" and the "us.""

He believed that when people stopped growing themselves, the relationship would be at risk of declining or dying.

"That sounds good on paper, though I have another concern. We are extremely opposite in a lot of ways. You seem to organize the details of life and follow your plans. I tend to create plans in my mind, though my life unfolds a bit more spontaneously. You are an engineer, so I'm guessing you are precise and efficient. I am a mother re-inventing myself and have never made the same meal twice, nor do I ever intend to." I was practicing some really scary open communication. I needed to show myself that I could step up my game of finding myself.

Mike smiled. "If I was interested in spending time with someone like myself I would install mirrors around my home. I'm not looking for someone like me. I like you." And with that, he gave me a kiss and asked if he could call me after work.

Around the same time, Jonathan had met a woman named Pamela. She also worked at Engineering Systems Inc., and at this point I had only met her once in the driveway of the house where Jonathan and I used to live. I was going over to pick up the boys and take them back home with me for the next week.

"I am so sorry," Pamela said, coming out to greet me. "Zachary fell out of his wheelchair and has a giant goose egg on his forehead."

I looked, and it was the biggest bump I had ever seen on a kid's head.

"He looks fine. Thanks for telling me about it. In a strange way, I would rather Zachary get a few bumps on his body and a few rips in his jeans, than living a life of sedation and boredom."

I found myself hoping and wishing that Pamela would bring new support to Jonathan, so that he would be happy. I wanted him to be happy. I wanted him to be happy, and I wanted to be free to be more of myself instead of continuing to fail in making him happy.

The following year, Jonathan and Pamela married, though Jonathan never mentioned it to me. The boys were strictly informed to never talk about their life at Jonathan and Pamela's house. So, I just acted like cut-off was a normal and healthy way to communicate with each other.

As we dated into June, Mike and I started to get to know each other in different ways. One particularly warm afternoon, I asked him if he could help me haul trash to the dump and replace a light fixture outside the front door. The boys were with their dad, and I had hauled a bunch of crap out of the backyard to the driveway. Mike showed up 20 minutes early, and I was my usual 20 minutes late, so I was already feeling 40 minutes behind schedule. He gave me a kiss hello, started tossing branches, boxes, and junk Michelle had helped me sort into the back of his truck. "You ready?"

"Yup."

"Why don't you grab a roadie?"

"Okay." I thought long and hard about this, and then asked, "Where is it?"

"A roadie?"

"Yeah—where do I find it?"

"It's a beer in your refrigerator."

It didn't seem like a good time for me to explain I had never done this before. So, I grabbed my first roadie, we split it in the driveway, then went to the dump.

Later that afternoon, I mentioned that I had a fixture outside the front door that needed to be replaced. He played it cool and waited to see if I was going to offer him anything. I said, "This is actually really important, so forget dinner, how about this. I will do any ONE thing for you in exchange for you replacing the outdoor fixture."

"Anything?" He had a mischievous grin on his face.

I went through a quick mental checklist of what Mai would whisper in my ear. "He'll probably just want yous to wash his truck topless." So, I said, "There are three rules: I will do anything privately, it has to be done this year, and you can't tell anyone about it."

"Let me see if I have this right. If I replace this fixture, you will do any one thing for me as long as it is private, it will happen this year, and I don't tell anyone about it."

I hesitated, mustered all my courage, and then blurted, "Yes."

Mike got the tools, removed the broken fixture. He gave me a smile, installed the new $9.79 outdoor light fixture from the clearance aisle at Builder's Square, and then sat down. I sat beside him on the wooden bench of the front porch. I snuggled up a little bit close and told him how much I appreciated him doing this. I was also feeling anxious to get this next conversation over with.

Finally I said, "Okay—so let's get down to business. What do you want me to do?"

He said, "Vote Republican in the upcoming elections. You can pull the curtain behind you, it happens in six months, and I won't tell anyone."

There was something unusually comforting when the boys and I visited Mike's home in Bellvue. He lived on 16 acres in a small rectangular home surrounded by a backdrop of tall sandstone rocks that glowed brilliant orange and red when illuminated by the sun rising or setting. The rocks formed a majestic ridge along the entire back property line. I had never seen a home in such an exquisite natural setting. The simple house was celadon green with turquoise trim, and the matching green-colored barn was slightly larger than the house. Mike's land looked like a miniature version of Sedona, AZ, home of internationally acclaimed yoga, art, musical festivals, and spiritual retreats. He had bought it from a woman who was a paraplegic, so there was a ramp from the gravel driveway up to the screen door on the front porch.

Mike was comfortable around both boys, and we established clear boundaries. Due to the hostility Jonathan showed toward me, Mike had clear boundaries. We agreed he would be my ally and supporter, though not be in a parenting or disciplinarian role. He helped Taylor build a small rocket, talked about sports, and showed him tips about how to be safe around horses. In his own spare time before we met, he had volunteered at a local 10K race to partner with a young woman in a wheelchair who wanted to race. Mike would offer Zachary Go-Gurt snacks, tell him jokes, read stories, and bring his dog Kasey to play. Sometimes, Mike would ask Zachary to watch a football game with him and then nod off, snoring on the couch. I could hear Zachary giggling because, just like Taylor said, guys seemed to think it was funny when people made noises with their body..

Pioneering this relationship was the biggest adventure of my life so far. As an extrovert who felt empty, deserted, and secluded during these years, I was a good candidate to cultivate more of my inner landscape. Mike helped continue the journey into non-verbal prompts that Zachary's birth had started six years previously. Some people say when the student is ready, the teacher will come, and he did.

Mike had an interest in tango dancing and some experience. I had actually listed dance lessons as a side note on my Costa Rican list. I did not dance at the time, though I really wanted to. It wasn't long before I saw how tango could be a metaphor for relationships. I, as the woman, was in charge of establishing the heart-to-heart connection during the dance. Mike's role was to navigate the outside world of the dance floor. We learned how the entire dance was improvisation yet with total precision. Each step was considered a syllable. We would put syllables together to form words, and words to form sentences, and sentences to form paragraphs. So, the instructors showed us a series of syllables, and then our focus was to feel the music and without any words, connect, listen, feel, string simple steps together, and dance.

It was erotic, stimulating, exhausting, sensual, and grueling. How could anything feel so encompassing and demanding without the use of language? Sometimes this was romantic. Other times, it was awkward. Later in our relationship, we took a private tango dance lesson. Our instructor, Carley, was an accomplished dancer and art teacher. To begin the one-hour lesson, she turned on La Cumparsita, tango's most famous dance song, to observe us. Within moments, she abruptly turned off the music and wagged her finger at me:

"Why do you accommodate him so much?"

"Ugh...."

"You must be more confident."

"Okay."

"Give him more attitude. You must surround him—not away or into him."

"Are you talking about the way I dance or the way I show up in our relationship?"

"Yes."

Another lesson in the power of non-verbal cues was taking horseback-riding lessons. Mike was an endurance horseback rider and competed in 25- and 50-mile races. He owned horses and asked if I had any interest in taking lessons. He had experience teaching a woman he had dated how to ride and found out later it was better to let someone else give instructions. For my birthday I got a series of dressage riding lessons. The instructor was approachable and friendly, and she put a lot of attention on how I was showing up to connect and be with the horse. Many of our lessons were focused on noticing my mental images resulting in an inner awareness of both my horse and myself. Later Mike gave me a book with a similar philosophy called "Centered Riding" by Sally Swift. Unlike traditional teachers, this author and my teacher pioneered an approach to riding that stressed "soft eyes," breathing, centering, and balance. These were the building blocks of riding and even racing competitively that used z-e-r-o language.

I was learning the power of silence, non-verbal cues, breathing, and applying these concepts to in my own life. I thought I was managing my stress in healthy ways. Even so, I was having bouts where my airway would shut down in the middle of the night. This had been happening before Zachary was born, and had I assumed it was just a real bad case of allergies. As the years passed, I tried more allergy medications and "doing" more things to reduce stress. I had a high drive to conquer challenges, so I could certainly take care of this terrible inconvenience called "not breathing in the middle of the night." This was a happy time in my life, though I was still stressed about my future and the future for my boys. There were so many unknowns and increased feelings of hostility from Jonathan, who lived less than a mile away.

I poured out my feelings in a journal and then threw the pages in the trash. I walked short, quick, fast distances with the boys in a Little Tikes Explorer Wagon for Two. I did everything I could, though I continued to struggle to find my breath, often between midnight and 4:00AM. I didn't tell Mike about it, and it never occurred to me to tell a doctor. Each time it happened, I felt embarrassed that I couldn't fix my own problem. I hated feeling like a high-maintenance person with a lot of problems. Each time my airway shut down, I would bargain with myself, God, and all the fears in my head that I would do anything to stop it, and then by morning pretend like it had never occurred.

CHAPTER 8

TAKING RISKS PROFESSIONALLY

To me, a sense of belonging was better than any drug addict's high, though I couldn't take a pill and mandate this feeling. This insight was painful because as a mom, I could tell how often this was missing for me, for each of my sons, and even us as a family. I couldn't figure out how to allow other people to be true to themselves and me be true to myself when they would see Zachary for the first time in his little wheelchair, Taylor darting off in another direction, and me pretending like I wasn't about to melt down. On my best days I could create a blink of a sense of belonging among the three of us, though the razor edges of isolation cut when we navigated daily living.

I started to develop some mantras for us. I told myself and the boys that the world was waiting for us, though we had to find the courage to show up each day. So, when Taylor was five and strapping his backpack over this T-shirt to walk to kindergarten, I would stand on the front ramp and say, "Remember to take a risk today!" I didn't want Taylor to grow up feeling either he or his brother was fragile in any way.

At the time, I needed checklists to help me manage the chaos of developing my career, managing medical appointments, documenting seizure activity, pureeing fresh vegetables, dealing with a complex shared-custody arrangement that was not working well for me or the boys, spending time with Mike, paying bills, returning phone calls, scheduling coaching calls, cleaning the bathroom, and moving clothes from the washer to the dryer on the same day.

As the lists got longer and more cumbersome, I started figuring out a checklist that would lift us up and create energy rather than leaving me feeling like I had not accomplished anything at the end of the day. That was the beginning of what later become our 5-Step Family Formula. It was a deliberate way for us to get focused and notice where we were putting our attention. Our daily formula was something like this:

- Dream BIG.
- Be still.
- Take daily action.
- Give thanks.
- Prepare to receive…because something good is happening.

During this time, my parents asked the boys and me to go skiing. I used to ski as a little girl, though I had not done so in years. I liked the idea of going, just because it gave my mental chatter a moment of normalcy.

The plan was for us to carpool with my parents and sisters over to Crested Butte and watch everyone ski. The boys and I could make a few snowballs, drink hot chocolate somewhere, and quite frankly that would be a full day. I wasn't sure how accessible the area would be for Zachary's wheelchair, but my hope was that we could just get outside and get around.

The first day, we settled into a shared room at the Mountaineer Square, a lodge just steps from the ski lifts. Taylor was excited to be at the hotel, and my mom and sister offered to watch him. Zachary and I went outside for a little walk. I noticed an office with some kind of welcome sign and a picture of someone in an adaptive ski. I figured we could stop in to make some small talk. I was growing some confidence in talking with people who were interested in outdoor adaptive recreation. The conversations were usually upbeat and energizing. We rolled inside to just scope it out. What happened next caught me completely off guard.

"Hello," I said to the young man behind the glass display counter.

"Howdy, folks, and welcome. My name is Blake, and who do we have here? What's your name, sport?"

Silence.

"Looks like you are in the right place, because we are getting geared up for our afternoon lessons." Blake came out from behind the counter and squatted down so that he was slightly lower than Zachary's eyes. He was brown-eyed, tall, about thirty years old. He had curly blond hair to his shoulders and was wearing a red ski instructor jacket and goggles on his forehead. "The snow is fantastic today, and we are going to have a blast. Do you have some warm gear?"

I interrupted: "Excuse me. We aren't here to ski. Zachary has severe cerebral palsy and a major seizure disorder and…"

Blake didn't seem to hear me. He walked away and got a clipboard.

"We'll need a little information about—uhh, what did you say this skier's name is?"

"Zachary. His name is Zachary."

I looked at the registration form on the clipboard. It just had some ordinary questions like his name, height, weight, level of experience, and other ordinary stuff.

"Zachary, you picked a great day to get out on the slopes with us. Henry, Charlotte, and I are the instructors, and we are going to have a blast out there."

Blake asked if Zachary had layers of non-cotton clothing, snow pants, a ski jacket, and warm mittens. He asked Henry to come join us. They seemed to have unprecedented confidence in themselves. Given it was Zachary's first time skiing, they pulled out a mono-ski. Blake described a method where Zachary would sit in a bucket-style seat with a single ski underneath him. They could strap some outriggers onto Zachary's hands so he could help guide himself, and the instructors would ski beside and in front of him with a rope system.

I can still remember feeling a sense of awe. I was so used to carrying the torch of hope for my small family of three and was even starting to carry hope for other people who felt marginalized or off their game. But the sheer enthusiasm of these instructors quietly thrilled me.

I was trying to quickly re-organize myself and get up to speed with this new conversation. The only thing that came out of my mouth was, "Do you have a bunny slope for us? Zachary really hasn't ever skied before."

Blake's response was clear: "You can ski anywhere you'd like. Henry, Charlotte, and I will be taking him up the Red Lady Express Lift. It's a quad chairlift that will take the four of us to the top. Lessons start in 90 minutes. Can Zach meet us back here in an hour?"

Blake squatted down, shook Zachary's hand, and said, "Glad to meet you, dude. Let's go do some skiing."

As we got Zachary's wheelchair turned around to navigate back through the ski shop, Charlotte mentioned that I could hop on the quad lift behind them and keep up.

"As Zachary's instructors, we'll be completely focused on getting him out on the slopes to have a good time and conquer some vertical feet together. You're welcome to join, though it's not necessary. We are going to have a blast."

In all my efforts to dream big, it had not even occurred to me that there were other people out there also with big dreams. We were crossing paths with people who had BIGGER dreams than we, and in this case, our job was to get dressed, give thanks, and go ski a mountain of possibilities!

Back in Fort Collins, reality resumed its dizzying pace. One of my Big Dreams was for our family to feel connected, cohesive, and kicked back. I wondered what it could be like to not be in motion and exhausted a-l-l t-h-e t-i-m-e. I was not naturally wired this way. I can honestly remember taking photos during Taylor's birthday, Zachary's birthday, Easter, and the last day of school and telling myself, "Just take one photo so that when we look back on our lives, there will be proof that we did give it a whirl and try to live an ordinary life." I did know that when Zachary and I went to yoga class together, something was different, so I started to imagine how to create a "yoga date" for our family at home without literally getting on a mat. So one late, chaotic afternoon I asked if they were up for table time. I said it was fun, easy, and we could do it together. The directions were simply:

1. Spend time after dinner each weekday.

2. Bring your homework, storybook, bills to pay or something else to the table.

3. Sit beside each other and do whatever we wanted at the table.

4. Imagine this is an easy chore.

5. Have fun: It doesn't sound like much, though it's important.

Thus "Table Time" was born. This structured 10–20 minutes removed any need to nag them about homework, it gave me a routine way to look through backpacks for notes from teachers, let the boys open mail and pay bills with me, and even allow for an inhale and exhale.

These extremely ordinary moments became a foundation for something I later understood to be an extraordinary life. Our ability to feel purpose, feel hope, and feel loved was the platform for all the good stuff that was unfolding for us. Still, at the time, as I was working hard to re-establish my new sense of a career, raising the boys, and managing the home, I was isolated. I did not belong to a team at work. I did not feel a sense of belonging with any adults at home. I was yearning for a social life where I could feel connected, yet also be invisible. I did not want to get to know anyone, and I didn't want anyone to get to know me. My relationship with Mike was growing, though I was hypersensitive about getting my own legs solid underneath me, rather than collapsing into him. I had a mental Life Wheel sizzling in my head, and the romance needle was climbing. The friends, health, fun, community sections of my life had sparks of hope.

I had now finished my coach training, coach certification, and was taking a one-year experiential, innovative leadership program funded by the Colorado Department of Education. At the same time, I was working full-time with The Coaching Project, listening to the feedback of participants and applying the new knowledge I was gaining. It was "guaranteed to help participants identify and break through self-perceived limits and put you on the road to a deeper and richer expression of yourself as a leader." The whole focus was to assist participants to connect with the essence of our own unique leadership style and journey. It was about getting in touch with our natural strengths and learning how to bring that authentic power of "self-expression" into all areas of life.

The timing was either the best or the worst because I still felt so ashamed of being a divorced mom. I felt ashamed to talk about the exhaustion of raising Zachary in a world that did not have natural supports in place for him. Throughout the leadership training, we were required to give voice to our hopes and dreams, immediately followed by the fears and feelings that stopped us from realizing them. There was no place to hide. There was no tolerance for talking about superficial things. Before we could lead others, we were required to do a deep dive into our own lives. We were required to be vulnerable and walk through these feelings into new actions and new possibilities. My shame of leaving a marriage with two young children ran deep. I felt guilty that I couldn't provide for the lifestyle I thought we would have, and I felt embarrassed that I had agreed to this—there was no one to blame. The entire first training session was called Creating from Self. The session focused exclusively on the premise that "We all carry a self-protecting framework of beliefs and limitations that keep us disconnected from our fundamental purpose, innate strengths, and gifts." I was surprised to hear accomplished professionals express moments of not feeling good enough in their roles and their feelings of doubt about living a life more attuned with their values. I was beginning to feel hopeful that the comfort I felt in The Coaching Project could broaden, and I could expand my confidence and work more strategically beyond people impacted by disabilities.

The next three training sessions were about creating from others, creating from space, and creating from everything. We were introduced to an incredibly rich set of coaching tools that could be applied in any organization or any industry. I was absorbing this whole idea of leadership through a coaching mindset and also gaining momentum in plotting my career. I was in the early stages of having a vision to work among organizations to provide individual and group coaching to people at no cost. Just like people in the workplace had access to paid time off and health insurance at no cost or a discounted rate, I had visions of a world where people could access conversations that practiced coaching skills.

So, upon my graduation from the one-year leadership program, I decided to put all my energy into pursuing this vision. I wanted to give back to the world that had somehow offered me a thread to hold onto during Zachary's diagnosis and then my divorce. I started by applying to be a coach trainer at The Coaches Training Institute, a national coach training program. I gathered my pennies, booked an airline ticket, and flew myself to the corporate office in San Rafael, California for the two-day interview. Mike had encouraged me to bring my full self, so I did.

There were nine of us engaged in the interview process, with five interviewers rotating through various activities. I felt a rush of connection between my inner sense of self and the interview activities we had to complete. I couldn't believe how nervous I felt. I wanted the job badly.

I couldn't believe how alive I felt, though I was engaging without any masks, completely naked and true to myself.

The conversations we had were all about what impact we wanted to have in the world, how we wanted to go about living this one precious life, and how willing we were to make some of the most important decisions of our lives, rather than falling asleep and living someone else's life. Some of my fellow interviewees were extremely playful and bold. One had a fearless sense of how to grow a multimillion-dollar company; one felt a calling to provide coaching to the leadership teams of convents from her faith across the nation; another had visions of establishing a lakeside retreat for entrepreneurs; others were charging ahead with a desire to coach executives of hi-tech companies; others did not have a plan yet radiated a confidence they were going somewhere.

By the end of the second day, the nine of us sat in a line of metal chairs in the small, sterile auditorium. The five interviewers asked us to get up in front of them one at a time to answer a series of questions. The mood had dramatically shifted. The questions were direct. The silence was distracting, and the volume of the chatter in my head became louder than usual.

A short, middle-aged man looked my way. "Sandy, please step to the front of the room."

I gathered all my values, intelligence, and personal convictions and approached the long table.

"If you are selected to be a national trainer, are you willing to end each of your classes by declaring to the number of coaching clients you have?"

The question caught me off guard. Why were they asking me this? In a flash, I knew why. They wanted me and all trainers to end each class by bragging about how many private paying clients we had. It made business sense to inspire participants by suggesting they could make big money on this career path, though I had bigger visions.

I scrambled for a moment and started to explain that I never wanted to take a penny from an individual client. I wanted to engage organizations to purchase individual and group coaching as a differential investment for their staff, customers, clients, etc.

The man asked me the question again. I was stumped. Didn't I just explain that I had bigger visions than that?

"You are a strong candidate," he said, after I stood there some moments in awkward silence. "We recommend you spend the evening finalizing your answer to this question. Tomorrow morning, we will ask you again. If you say yes, you will be a final candidate as a national trainer. If you say no, we will say, 'Thank you' and 'Goodbye.'"

I walked back to my little motel room and sobbed. How could I possibly experience the euphoria of speaking my personal conviction and simultaneously be told 'Goodbye'?

I sat on the edge of my bed, which smelled like moth balls. The same room that had given me hope in the morning now felt cramped, dark, and depressing. I picked up the phone and called Mike.

"Hey! How did it go? Mike sounded unusually energetic.

I held back my tears. "Remember I said I wanted to be true to myself?"

"Yeah—of course."

"Well, it's not working out so well." My quiet tears turned into sobs. "If I stay true to myself, I am not going to get picked for the job. If I tell them what they want to hear, I might get picked for my dream job."

Silence.

"How the fuck is this supposed to work?" It was the first time I ever said the "F" word to Mike and only the second or third time I had said it in my whole life. "How can I work all this time practicing how to lead with my instincts, imagining ways to transform lives, when I can't even get a job?" I watched a stupid bird outside the window hop from branch to branch.

"What's most important to you?" Mike finally said.

"I want to bring coaching into organizations so that people in the workplace can reconnect with their purpose. I want people to feel lifted up like I personally experienced with a coach. I want to be part of the solution so leaders can find their path to transform the experience of each of their customers, clients, and patients they work with each day. I want to teach coaching skills to leaders, so they can literally tap into the unlimited potential in the workplace. I want this to be available to everyone—not only people with extra income. Think about it: I would have never had access to a coach if I had had to pay for it." My voice trailed off into a sense of hopelessness. "Crap. Never mind."

"You have a vision, Sandy. Be true to yourself."

"I don't think it really works that way, Mike. I need a career path, and I need to pay my bills. This just sucks."

Mike was practical and succinct. "You are good at what you do, Sandy. I think they need you more than you need them. Get some sleep tonight, tell them your idea in the morning, and then come home. I miss you."

That night I didn't sleep a wink. I convinced myself that this was just one of those moments where you get tested, though it all works out in the end. I felt more relaxed when I walked in the next morning. I had rehearsed my vision in less than 20 words: "I have a vision of establishing coaching clients and teaching coaching skills to achieve organizational breakthroughs by invoicing organizations." I was focused and ready.

We were called in for our final interview. This time, it was a woman asking the dreaded question: "Are you willing to end each of your coach training classes by declaring to the number of coaching clients you have?"

I started to speak my 20-word vision, and then she politely interrupted me. "Thank you. Goodbye."

I was in need of a happy distraction from the failed trip to California. Once again, The Coaching Project helped me to my feet. Susan, Elizabeth, Barbara, and I buckled down to write another grant application to continue The Coaching Project and take it to the next level.

I came back to the CDE application process and realized the irony of my recent experience. As director of The Coaching Project, I was able to do the exact work I wanted to do. The grant allowed us to create new ways of designing and developing a leadership curriculum—and individuals *didn't need to pay for it.*

We worked hard to identify language that captured the spirit of "coaching" and "leadership." We partnered with organizations across Colorado to catapult our goals into action. We developed better materials, included an orientation for people prior to each workshop, and even got a toll-free business line for our individual and group coaching sessions. We developed pre and post surveys to measure impact and document outcomes for individuals and teams.

It was amazing to me how effortless it was to bring these core coaching communication skills into a world that had historically felt marginalized and burdened with heaviness. We were engaging with clients as people first. We were following an award-winning blueprint to guide conversations and meetings to unleash more human potential. We were showing how people who practiced these coaching communication skills were achieving breakthrough outcomes and experiencing more fulfillment in their professional roles and personal lives.

It wasn't until years later that I really understood what Carlos Castaneda meant by what he called the Cubic Centimeter of Chance: "All of us, whether or not we are warriors, have a cubic centimeter of chance out in front of our eyes from time to time. The difference between an average man and a warrior is that the warrior is aware of this, and one of his tasks is to be alert, deliberately waiting, so that when his cubic centimeter pops out, he has the necessary speed, the prowess to pick it up."

Grace and God had been working behind the scenes to create this cubic centimeter of chance for me and our family. It was almost like this grand invitation was trying to reveal itself. The combination of Zachary's birth in 1991, IDEA Part C public policy going into place in 1993, Taylor's birth, the opportunity to serve as CICC cochair and participate in coach training had all come together. Still, on some days I wondered if I had enough of the warrior spirit in me to get out of bed.

I needed to find a job that provided access to steady health insurance and benefits without the risk of losing them in the event The Coaching Project contract was not renewed. In the back of my mind, I was scared to death that at any moment (with no backup plan), the boys and I could be on the streets. I did not have any contingency plans for anything; we were getting by one day at a time. We didn't go to the movies, and the boys didn't attend camp. Taylor played with the crawdads in the creek across the street and had water-balloon fights in the backyard with friends from school. We sucked on frozen grapes on the front porch and fed stale bread to the ducks at the end of the street. I put together a bird-watching kit with a book from the library and a stack of blank white paper stapled together. We took the public bus to the public library ONCE, and I swore I would never do that again because it took us a clumsy 4.5 hours, allowing only 20 minutes at the library.

Mike had I were now dating more seriously, though we had both adopted this philosophy of maintaining a "you"—"me"—and "us." So, I was working diligently at finding a next step for my career so I could keep supporting the boys and myself.

In the fall of 2000, Mike and I drove to Boulder. We had season tickets to the CU Buffalo football games, and when the boys were with their dad, I would join Mike at the games. This was his alma mater, and it was a whole new world for me. When we tailgated before each game, I was shocked to see how much people liked to talk about sports. I had never really been exposed to this before. The men and women at these games really bonded over sports, sport, sports. His group of friends adopted me even though I was not particularly experienced at screaming, hollering, eating fatty foods, or smoking game-day cigars.

On this particular drive, I was deeply engrossed in completing a four-page paper application for a corporate coaching team. It would be another chance to interview for the work I had been preparing myself for. A few weeks later, I learned that I got the interview. I spent three weeks preparing in every way I could. I went to our local Foothills Fashion Mall and asked the clerk at Macy's what "business casual" meant. I collected paper coupons and bought three new outfits. I settled on a bright-pink cardigan sweater set to match a pair of pink plaid crop pants, a turquoise cardigan sweater set to match a pair of khaki pants and a simple wrap dress in black. I studied models of coaching and kept fighting with the gremlins in my head. I memorized the itinerary outlining the interview process. Our schedule would include coaching, software training, learning the company's leadership model and networking in restaurants along the ocean. I bought a another round-trip airline ticket to California to go through the interview process once again, but this time, after a three-day, competitive session, I was offered a position.

This new role as a coach for a global training company opened a great big door of possibilities for me. I could take the next baby step in actualizing my vision of how people could get access to coaching conversations without paying for it. This company introduced us to a web platform and Coach Management System (CMS). It had an incredibly comprehensive process to train all of the new coaches and a step-by-step plan to get us set up for our international coaching engagements. It literally was a dream come true that I had not even dreamed of yet!

In December 2000 I signed a contract for employment. I was assigned to coach directors and executives in the industries of finance, global communication, sales and customer service in Europe, Asia, and the Japanese-Pacific Rim. Most of the coaching engagements focused on supporting leaders to build more cohesive teams, increase productivity, and become more effective leaders, especially of global teams.

I felt ready. I was certified, credentialed, experienced, and had even put together some good stuff in three-ring notebooks to use as resources. Much of my coach training was about uncovering the "old rules" people lived by and guiding conversations to generate "new rules" to live by. My notes were stellar. My dreams were about to bust open and take off.

My first executive call was scheduled for 1:00PM. By about 9:30AM, I wanted to cancel. I wanted to explain I was the wrong person. Given the choice, I would have preferred to clean dirty diapers with my bare hands than follow through with this ludicrous idea.

The phone rang. I picked it up before the ring even finished. "Hello."

"Hello, is this Sandy?"

I was hoping he had a conflict and was going to request we reschedule. Instead, he was gracious and professional.

Eventually, I found my breath, and together we found our way. By the end of the call, I was so surprised. I was surprised that the basic and advanced coach training made such a difference.

Each coaching conversation was 60 minutes and had a beginning, middle, and end. Each coaching engagement had a beginning, middle, and end, which lasted about six months. The structure sounded so basic, yet each conversation was profoundly intimate and individualized. As I coached executives, I could witness how people were able to anchor themselves into new ways of thinking. They discovered new ways of sharing their vision and strategic thinking; they resolved conflict in new ways and collaborated with renewed confidence. As leaders rediscovered their own sense of purpose and meaning, they were able to support their teams to transcend barriers that had limited growth. I was stunned at how I could be the same mom, the same coach, using the same skills and witness leaders dramatically improve performance, teamwork, and results.

I was witnessing something spiritual. I was noticing how the questions we ask each other determine what we find. I was discovering that asking people "What do you want to happen?" allowed something to begin to shift. Coaching skills allowed me to help myself and others imagine the future, and then plan and equip ourselves to live into that future with new energy and purpose.

PART III

Zachary & Taylor flying frequently. Taylor often flew solo.

CHAPTER 9

THE NIGHTMARE BEGINS

In the winter of 2002 it was time to complete the redetermination paperwork for Zachary to access the Children's Extensive Services (CES) waiver. I had a great big insight. Rather than filling in the complex bureaucratic application with all of the language that characterized him as a hopeless and helpless toddler, I would describe Zachary through the lens of his abilities. I felt satisfied and pleased with myself that I could use more creative and positive language to represent my young son.

Instead of saying he has cerebral palsy with frequent seizures, I wrote, "Zachary is a young boy who likes to spend time outdoors with a few adaptations." Instead of saying he couldn't feed himself, dress himself, brush his teeth, or be potty trained, I said, "Zachary likes spicy food pureed, needs support for his daily care, and wears underpants." And, rather than admitting my son could not roll over, move either arm across the midline of his body, turn or bend over, I wrote, "Zachary is physically active at the local recreation center, health club, neighborhood pool, and scout activities."

The consequences were clear. Zachary was denied access to all CES benefits. This meant that, for the next year, any people who supported

Zachary in our home were either assigned new families to work with, or I needed to find a way to privately pay for their services, which averaged about $35/hour. I immediately called the Colorado State Department of Human Services. I needed to explain my grand experiment—that his needs were the same or perhaps even more intense, however, I was practicing a new way of describing him as "less broken."

I looked up the names of people to whom I could desperately explain my error. After numerous false leads, I reached a woman who could potentially help. "Hello, hello, my name is Sandy Scott, and I am so glad you can take my call."

"What can I do for you, Ms. Scott?"

"My son Zachary has been denied the CES waiver to assist him to live a typical life, and he has a whole lot of significant and profound disabilities. He can't crawl, roll over, climb, kick, walk, or run. He can't say his name or age, say a short sentence, or even speak a word. He can't scribble, put his own food in his mouth, or drink from a cup. He requires someone to roll him over during the night, sit him up in his wheelchair when he leans forward too far, reposition him during the day, puree his food so there are no chunks, and give him tiny sips of fluid through a sippy cup.

"Someone needs to be watching him at all times because he has seizures around the clock and can't ask for help; he can choke at any time and aspirate. His needs are very high, and I made a big mistake in completing his CES waiver through my eyes, not the eyes of the state funders. May I please, please, please ask for a redo? I will drive the new application down to your Denver office tomorrow morning and hand-deliver it to you in person." I gasped for air and hoped I wouldn't have to repeat this again. I had already made this plea to six other people in different agencies. And it wasn't even eleven o'clock. "Actually, am I even talking to the right person in the right office?"

"Yes," the kind woman said. I took a breather and felt relieved. "I am sorry your son was denied services. We do have an appeals process in which you can attend an appeal hearing to defend your position. In the meantime, I can also provide you with the phone numbers for a local disability agency that may be able to help you."

I felt overwhelmed at the thought of both pursuing the appeals process and managing Zachary's care without the CES. I immediately called people I knew from the CIC Council. I learned the appeals process could take up to a year and would be even more cumbersome than the original application. I was feeling like the hill I had been climbing had just turned into an impossible mountain. My path suddenly was one of belaying steep rocks and crossing glaciers and crevasses without the crampons, ice axes, or other critical equipment.

That winter was long as I wondered how we could go forward without any formal assistance with Zachary. Seeking distraction one evening, I turned the radio to the country music station. Garth Brooks was singing "Do What You Gotta Do." As I gave Zachary a sip of water, it dribbled down his shirt, and I started to make quesadillas for dinner.

I thought about the moments in my past that gave me hope and helped me to re-orient my focus. One was when my dad and I took a motorcycle trip to visit the national parks. We trailered our two bikes from New Jersey to Colorado and then explored the West by motorcycle. It was a memorable adventure where we bonded even though we rode separately. So, without much thought or hesitation, I wondered if I could recreate that father-daughter trip with a mother-son trip.

"Taylor, if we could go camping anywhere in the USA, where would you want to go this summer?"

We had a world map scotch taped to the wall and a 12" × 15" Rand McNally spiral-bound road atlas hanging off the corner of the kitchen table. Eight-year-old Taylor flopped the two-page map of the USA wide open on the kitchen table. "To the Cal-i-forn-ia," he said brightly.

"What do you want to do there?"

"Just the fun stuff that happens in Cal-i-forn-ia."

I asked him to set the table while I grated cheese for the typical meal we seemed to eat every other night. "Well then, after dinner, how about if you start mapping the route you want to follow? We'll have 10 days to camp anywhere you want."

"Sewr-iously?"

So, Taylor spent the winter months addressing envelopes to Chambers of Commerce up and down the Cal-i-forn-ia coast. As we got packages in the mail, he designed our trip from start to finish. His general plan was to make a loop to the south, from Colorado to Bryce and Zion National Park, and then up the coast of California and loop back home through Mount Rushmore and Steamboat Springs.

I didn't exactly know what I would do with Zachary, but planning the trip infused hope about our future during the cold dark nights. I wanted to start finding more ways to spend one-on-one time with each of the boys and up our game as to how we spent time as a family.

During early spring, we stayed active. We managed a day of skiing at Copper Mountain, splurged with an overnight hotel room at the Denver Embassy Suites for spring break, all while Taylor mapped our first mother-son trip.

In March, I had an abnormal pap smear. My physician said not to be concerned, just to come back in six weeks to repeat the exam. I tried not to worry, though I dreaded the feeling of the unknown. I had health insurance through June 30th with my CDE contract, which I didn't know would be renewed or not. In late April, I repeated the pap smear and was scheduled for a follow-up appointment.

I parked my car outside the clinic and walked across the hot asphalt. I was writing a grocery list on the back of a deposit ticket from my check-book and another list of questions to ask Zachary's teacher at his upcoming IEP meeting. I had only about 15 minutes for this appointment and was feeling slightly agitated that we couldn't discuss the results on the phone. The office manager slid the glass door open and handed me a clipboard with papers to complete. I got checked in and waited in the small lobby of the sterile waiting room. The plants of the basement office were plastic, and the carpet was old. The ventilation was minimal and the lighting dim. I never noticed the dungeon-like feeling before and wondered if I should find a new ob-gyn doctor after this appointment.

"Your pap smear test results are abnormal again." Silence. The doctor was matter of fact.

"We will need to schedule a series of diagnostic procedures to determine the stage of your cervical cancer, blah, blah, blah."

I didn't hear anything else he said. When the appointment concluded, I walked to the front desk, stone faced. The clerk was polite and recommended some dates for the next appointment. As I walked to the car, I forgot about the grocery list, Zachary's IEP, or even the dates for the next appointment. I got into the car and sat in silence. I told myself it was not serious. I told myself I had a lot to do and needed to stay focused, keep eating well, get more sleep, walk more often, and stay connected to my kids. I needed to tell Mike and let go of anything that drained my energy.

This same week, Jonathan called. We rarely talked on the phone, and our formal emails were one to two sentences long.

"Pamela and I have decided to move to New Hampshire."

I shushed Taylor, who was singing loudly in the living room. "You're moving where?"

"We are moving to New Hampshire this summer. The boys can move with us or stay with you."

"Why are you moving? What do you mean moving? The boys can't be forced to move."

I felt a wave of panic wash over me. My heart raced, and my mind sprinted.

"We are moving, and I'll keep you informed of the actual move date."

"I don't understand. What the heck is in New Hampshire?"

"As I said, Pamela and I are moving and I'll keep you informed of the details." With a click, Jonathan hung up.

Within two months, my ex-husband and his new wife were ready to move 2,000 miles away to New Hampshire, where she was from, to be near her supportive family. Jonathan would telecommute and continue working for Engineering Systems Inc., where he and Pamela were both engineers. I went to every attorney and child advocate I could find to ask what the options were. I did not have access to any assistance to help me raise Zachary; my work was still on a contract basis. I was able to pay my bills, but I did not have any discretionary income to pay for providers to help me with Zachary. Without Jonathan's help, I didn't know how we could manage.

The conversation with my attorney, which I paid for in 15-minute intervals, was short:

"Can Jonathan really just move across the country, even if it's not best for the boys?"

"Yes, he can move."

"What about all of Zachary's medical needs? I'm not able to provide for all of his needs by myself. Doesn't Jonathan have to assist in taking care of Zachary's needs?"

"No. He has no additional responsibilities."

"I don't even have a stable job, or ways to support Zachary when I'm at work."

"He can leave the state and provide basic child support, or you can agree for him to take the boys with him to New Hampshire."

"He can what? What about meeting the boys' needs?"

"Sounds tough, Sandy. I'm sorry that's the way it is." Click, my attorney hung up.

Zachary was still having daily seizures, often during the middle of the night. It was time intensive to puree his food, spoon-feed him his meals, liquids, and medicines. He required the physical support of a baby compounded with complex medical needs 24/7.

The child advocates and attorneys all agreed: my ex-husband could leave the state. If I did not have the capacity to raise the boys alone, then I would need to let them go to New Hampshire with him.

I couldn't believe this was happening. I couldn't imagine what kind of mother would let her children go. Mike listened. He assured me that we would work through this together. In some ways I wanted him to just suit up in shining armor and ride a white horse up the driveway and save me. Instead, Mike reminded me that he was there to support my decision about what I thought was best for the boys. Mike did not take a stand on what I should do; rather, he was a practical sounding board about what I needed. Mike was a grounding force and spoke the unspoken. He was in more shock than I that a father would move out of state and disrupt his children's lives, especially since his new wife married him knowing his home, children, and career were established in Colorado.

I was overwhelmed with shame, disgrace, and fear for my children. I had been terribly judgmental of any mom who ever left her children when she had the option to raise them. Now, I was one of them.

I wanted to bribe, plea, beg for a redo and start this whole co-parenting relationship with Jonathan over again. One afternoon in May, I called him. "Is there anything I can say or do so they boys can stay in Colorado until they are 18?"

"Pamela and I are moving to New Hampshire this summer."

"Can we brainstorm some way to support the boys to stay here until I can stabilize my career?"

Silence.

"Jonathan. I am asking you to please help the boys to stay here in their neighborhood with the teachers, church, family, friends, physicians, and childcare providers they know. Would you help pay for childcare when Zachary has fevers or seizures and can't go to school? Or help pay for a companion to assist me in getting him to medical appointments so I can stay employed?"

"I am done talking about this. You can keep the boys, or they can move with us." The conversation was over before it even got started. The ground beneath me split open like the San Andreas fault, and I disappeared into the dark underground.

"Okay. Zachary and Taylor will move with you to New Hampshire."

"I'll email you the details." Click. The decision had been made.

I started to weep uncontrollably at odd moments and was not sleeping or eating. I alienated myself from friends and felt too ashamed to admit to the decision I had agreed to. I was scared to death if the boys stayed with me that we would begin a long, slow road toward poverty. I didn't ask Mike to financially take care of the boys and me. Mike was very invested in us, though he did not consider himself a replacement for their dad. I had a diagnosis of cancer, no secure job, and we had lost the CES waiver to cover Zachary's medical bills and daily care by certified nursing assistants. Mike had a terrible experience with marriage and divorce and said his philosophy was to do things out of love, not a legal contract. I was scared, though I valued our ability to openly talk about money, careers, religion, deal breakers, how to handle conflicts, and dreams.

Mike and I had made an agreement early on to divide all shared expenses 50/50. This meant I didn't need to ask him if we had enough money for me to buy a new dress, and Mike didn't need to ask me if we had enough money to buy a new tool. The idea was to be free of difficult financial conversations. Mike lived frugally. He saved aggressively and was on target to retire by age 58 using his own personal savings. We made decisions differently, spent money differently, yet loved each other fully.

Mike didn't want the boys to move to New Hampshire. He also didn't want to pick up the responsibilities that Jonathan could handle if he lived in Fort Collins until the boys turned 18. In fact, Mike's conviction was that Jonathan was wrong to even think of moving out of state given that our current parenting arrangement worked for Taylor, Zachary, and all of Zachary's special needs. Mike felt Jonathan was ignoring what was best for them.

In preparation for this unexpected major life transition, I scheduled a going-away party for each of the boys. We had 12 fifth-graders from our local elementary school get together for a ping-pong party to celebrate Zachary and his move to New Hampshire in late May as school was getting out. Another mom and I arranged for five third-graders to meet at our swimming pool across the street for a June pool party to celebrate Taylor and his move.

In the meantime, I had an ultrasound, MRI, and loop electrosurgical excision procedure to remove the cervical cancer cells. I had the procedures done while the boys were at Jonathan's house. I paid my co-payment and didn't tell anyone except Mike where I was going. I hated the idea of being such a high-maintenance person who seemed to be consistently leading a life of drama. I had no capacity to listen or support other people, and I didn't want to lose the girlfriends I had.

Michelle, our trusted childcare provider, offered us a tremendously discounted rate so I could afford for her to watch Zachary for a week while Taylor and I went on our trip. On June 1st we went over the details of Zachary's routine. Then we went over and over the details some more. Michelle knew Zachary well. Still, my heart was spinning, and I couldn't figure out if this trip was really good timing or really bad timing. What kind of mother would leave one of her kids behind to go on a road trip? I kept telling myself this was a healthy choice, as Taylor and I threw our camping gear into the little sports car we had rented.

As I slid into the driver's seat, I fought back tears while silently scolding myself to get it together. I needed to act happy. I needed to be nurturing and upbeat so that Taylor and I could have this one trip to remember. I needed Taylor to know that he was loved and everything was going to be all right. I would pretend the boys were not moving to New Hampshire when we got back.

We sat in the driveway, and I said, "Okay, when I back out, which direction do you want to go?"

I think Taylor thought I was kidding. I wasn't kidding.

I had spent all my energy on getting the basic essentials packed for our trip, the medications, and emergency information ready for Zachary and Michelle, and had worked extra hours so I could take off. I had not spent one minute looking at the map.

Taylor hesitated and then said, "Uh—go that way."

So, we went that way.

Taylor had layers of AAA maps spread across his lap. He organized our route, and I thought about the logistics for the upcoming evening. As we crossed the border into Utah, we drove into a hellacious sandstorm like something out of a science fiction movie with digital tsunamis made of sand. I instantly became a blind driver in the fast lane with no sense of what was in front, behind, or beside us. I couldn't see the hood of our car. I couldn't see the lines in the road, and I couldn't tell how to protect my son. I felt blindsided and unprepared for the situation—a metaphor for my life.

The storm stopped as quickly as it came.

I pulled off at the next exit and asked Taylor to pump the gas. I ran into the restroom because I was pretty sure I had peed on myself ever so slightly. When I came out, he was standing by the pump looking pretty in charge of the situation. Then he asked, "How do you work this machine?" And so, we started the journey needing each other in new ways.

We spent the night in Zion National Park, and Taylor used the camp stove to make dinner. We ate Dinty Moore beef stew and pop tarts, attended Ranger programs at the national parks, hiked up hidden canyons and said goodbye to Utah. Next, we said hello to Arizona, and Taylor directed me to drive the rim of the Grand Canyon. We set our tent up inside a tepee and got our passport books stamped at the next Ranger talk. We hiked a very narrow and difficult trail and spotted a California Condor with a wingspan of 9'5". There were only 57 worldwide.

The next morning, we awoke at 3:30AM. I suppose at home I would have felt obligated to say "Go back to sleep," but here we were in the flow of just doing whatever we were drawn to do. So, we looked each other in the eye, got up, took the tent down, and slowly pulled out. As we did, a giant moose was standing in the middle of the road.

We traveled to Las Vegas through the 123-degree Mojave National Preserve. Unfortunately, I had eaten onions the night before, which meant I had really bad gas. No sound effects, just obnoxious odors that filled the car for hours. Taylor couldn't decide which was worse, rolling down the windows or suffocating inside with air conditioning.

By the time we got to a secluded campsite at Sequoia National Park, we were exhausted from doing nothing. We bought some cherries at the roadside and noticed a sign that read: "Last bear break-in at this campground was 2 days." We ate quickly and then put our cooler, chap stick, baby wipes, food, trash, and toiletries in the bear box. Taylor had mastered setting up the tent independently each night. As I unrolled our sleeping bags, I noticed his journal entry for the day. We each kept a separate journal and whether we wanted to or not, had agreed to draw or write something about each day. Taylor's highlight was playing in the creek with his sneakers.

We visited the General Sherman Tree, tagged the largest living thing on earth, and we saw a mama bear and her cub. I thought about all the mother/son connections in the animal kingdom. I thought about my own mother/son connections and hoped I was doing an okay job raising my sons as individuals and as brothers.

The strangest part of the trip was my awareness of how guilty I felt walking on all different terrain. I realized that it would have been impossible for me to take Zachary across rocky trails, sandy campsites, and other uneven surfaces. I also realized that I needed to make sure Taylor got access to parts of the world that were not wheelchair accessible. I was struggling with how to adapt so that each of us got access to living a meaningful life.

We continued our trip to visit my college roommate. We ate burgers, watched lizards, walked Carmel Beach, and talked, talked, talked. We visited the Children's Discovery Museum in San Jose, and Taylor designed a stunt bike using computer-aided design to build a 20" spoked small, sturdy steel framed which was then rated "Killer" on the success meter. He got so energized he went on to design a roller coaster based on principles of physics using a bar-coded card, and we got to virtually ride it in a simulator.

Taylor and I both felt "done" with our trip, so we ended it early and buzzed home in a straight line from California to Colorado. A few days later was Taylor's 9th birthday. We celebrated with Scooby Doo napkins and a food fight with pasta in the back yard. Zachary and I gave him a hockey stick, and my sister took him out for ice cream.

We had Taylor's going-away party a few weeks later. I took pictures so I could tell myself I'd done my best: photos of Taylor playing with his friends, eating popsicles, cutting a sheet cake, and jumping off the diving board. I told the other parents we were prepared for our adventure together. I told them whatever I needed them to believe so that I didn't run away in tears.

The dreaded day came on Saturday, July 13, 2002. Jonathan came to pick up the boys after breakfast. I had asked Mike to stay in Bellvue that morning so I could devote all of myself to the boys amidst the sadness that consumed me. I told him that I would need him later to help me sort all the contradictory feelings.

Zachary, Taylor, and I walked out the door and stood at the top of the ramp. I held each of them tightly and told them they were going to meet amazing new friends. I choked on my own tears and told them how exciting their flight would be. I had packed a small care package for each of them and had already made little postcards with daily jokes ready to put in the mail each morning. Taylor plastered a pretend smile on his face, and so did I. As he got in the car and Jonathan loaded Zachary's wheelchair, I felt deep mourning. All the hope and skills I had learned from my coaching training seemed irrelevant and bogus.

I was empty as the car drove away, scared for them and their future and at a loss about my own. I was devastated that I'd brought them into this world and was now worried they would feel abandoned. I had designed my world around raising my sons, loving them, being there for them. I planned to be there to talk about Boy Scout projects, mend their jeans, walk them home from school—and now all that had been stolen.

CHAPTER 10

IN HELL

The state of Colorado required divorced parents to take parenting classes that provided clear information: answer kids' questions honestly and assist them in dealing with their own feelings. Don't pump them for information, and don't speak negatively about the other parent.

I completed the class and even took notes about key phrases to use, especially as it related to the boys transitioning into their new lives in New Hampshire. I offered them reassurance. I told them they would meet new friends, wonderful teachers, and have a new bedroom. In all honesty, I was also convincing myself that I was not losing my relationship with my kids.

I spent as many hours as I could coaching executives and saved every penny, nickel, and dime to fly out to see the boys. My gut instinct was to focus on the importance of ordinary moments. So, I developed my own daily rituals to keep our relationships alive. I tried practicing some of the coaching techniques I was using in my new coaching business. One sounded good, though it also felt pathetically simple. It was to ask myself a simple question: The Miracle Question.

Looking back I never put together how awkward it was to be coaching others on achieving their dreams while I was suffocating. Nonetheless, I started to write each morning as one way to quiet the saboteur heckling me for living such a divided life.

The Miracle Question is used in coaching to assist people to imagine their best future life and then take baby steps in that direction. So, I would get up in the mornings and write my response to these questions:

1. "Imagine that tomorrow morning I wake up and suddenly find that a magical transformation, a miracle, has taken place. My world would be just as I would like it to be, and I have resolved all my problems or come to terms with all the things that are bothering me. Describe what would be different, and what are the particular things that tell me that things have changed? Enter into as much detail as I can."

2. "What can I do that would help me to move even if in only a small way toward the new world I have described?"

I hated this exercise, but once I got started, I hated to stop. I poured my desires onto the page. I wrote about Zachary living in our everyday home with natural routines in the neighborhood. I imagined him having a schedule common to other boys his age. I imagined him attending our local neighborhood high school, going to prom, and graduating with Fort Collins peers. I imagined Taylor riding his bicycle on the trails of Fort Collins, building outdoor forts, clubhouses, and tree houses. I yearned to lallygag in the mornings and then go explore local art, music, and nature with the boys rather than compress our lives into three-day travel bytes. I wanted to make pancakes with chocolate chip smiley faces and divide household chores for the three of us to do. I wanted to have time to get bored, feel angry, say, "I'm sorry," and spend time offstage with the boys.

I wanted to invest in who they were and who they were becoming. I wanted time and space to not know… and then listen to what might emerge.

Mike and I were becoming more serious and decided to move in together. We had each been married and divorced and knew a thing or two about tying the knot. I did not want to have more children, and the current divorce rate was 60%. Mike proposed we commit to creating our life together, though avoid provisions in the tax code that could force us to pay more than single people. We updated our wills to reflect our partnership, got specific about how to cover our expenses, ensured big-ticket items were properly titled, and openly communicated our long-term hopes and dreams. We were fully invested in each other and our life as a couple/family. We talked about our future through both a practical and romantic lens.

We settled into his house, but I kept 1808 Centennial Road in the event the boys ever moved back. I needed to know that I could provide for them, and the cost of real estate in Fort Collins was increasing, so I decided to rent it. I told Mike I wanted and needed to use all of my vacation time to fly to New Hampshire or fly out there to pick them up and bring them home for the summers or holidays. He agreed it was critical for me to be active in their lives and offered to join me on some trips.

Mike and I each worked hard. In his spare time, Mike did chores on our 16 acres of pasture and worked with the horses. We joined a local health club, hiked in the local state park, biked along the local Spring Creek trail, and rode horses. We were usually in bed by 10:00PM and up before sunrise. I started to do yoga more regularly, though my airway would still randomly shut down when I was in a deep sleep. I would wake up in the dark of the night unable to breathe. Mike would either take me to the ER or sit beside me until I was able to relax and get air again.

I never did lash out at Jonathan, in part because I was afraid he would block me from spending time with the boys. As it was, he strictly forbade me from ever driving near their home. I have never understood the reason for this. I felt ashamed. I wondered what I was being punished for. I did know that he and Pamela had a daughter together, though Taylor was strictly instructed to never talk about his experiences in his other family so I didn't ask. It felt so out of step that I couldn't ask Taylor about his experiences at his new home. When I came to visit, Jonathan would give me the address of a convenience store parking lot where I was to pick up Taylor. I poured all of my energy into pretending that flying to another city, driving to another state, and meeting my nine-year-old son in a parking lot that smelled like diesel fuel was a typical way for a mother and son to connect.

During the fall, Taylor was signed up to play football. Taylor hated contact sports, and I could sense the stress in his world had continued to increase. Mike and I bought cheap tickets on Sept. 11th to go watch Taylor play. We showed up in Stratham and drove straight to pick him up and take him to our Hampton Inn Hotel room. On the night before the game, Taylor told us he felt sick. He had diarrhea and a stomachache. He got suited up for the game, though he didn't play. It was another reminder to me that something was wrong, yet I felt helpless to make it right.

During the same fall, Jonathan called. "I wanted to tell you that I am having a hard time taking care of Zachary."

"What's going on?"

"His needs are too complex, and even though Pamela is now a stay-at-home mom, we can't take care of him here."

"I understand it's hard. I am totally available to find out what resources there mirror the supports we had here in Colorado." I started pacing the floor, making a mental list of people I could start calling immediately.

"That won't be necessary. I found a place for him."

I couldn't believe what I was hearing. "You did what? Jonathan, you don't have to do this alone. I can fly out immediately and do the research to get the supports you want and need so Zachary can live with you in your home."

"We've already decided. He will live in a facility for kids with severe disabilities."

"Jonathan, that sounds terrible for Zachary! He has never even been away from either of us for more than a single night."

"I'll let you know Zachary's move-in date and address so you can visit him there. It's an hour-and-a-half north of here. You can look it up on a map." Click.

I was overwhelmed with shock and panic. To me, these institutions were nice buildings on the outside, while filled with dark secrets on the inside. I feared that any warehouse for people with disabilities would restrict his life experiences. I assumed that employees had high turnover or were desensitized and that Zachary would experience high variations in care. Guilt washed over me as I wondered if Zachary would lose his bright-eyed spirit and his sense of belonging to our family and friends. Even when I thought about a best-case scenario, I could not begin to imagine how a large organization could begin to tap the potential of a young child. In my heart, children needed to be among family and friends to grow and participate in their communities. The idea of living inside a self-made, giant organization filled me with horrors of Zachary being isolated from real life.

It was Christmas Eve. I flew from Denver to Manchester, MA, rented a car, and picked up Taylor at the appointed gas station. It was beyond disturbing to me that I couldn't drive by and let Taylor point out the window to his bedroom. Jonathan and I never had a conversation about this; he just sent an email to me telling me if I did not comply, he would get a restraining order on me. I obeyed without discussion. There trips were supposed to be about reducing stress and anxiety for the boys, not creating it. So, I picked up Taylor at our appointed gas station, and we drove to Keene, where Zachary was living.

Zachary started living in one institution, Crotched Mountain in Greenfield, NH, and then was moved to another one, Cedar Crest Center in Keene, NH. Each time I went to visit him, I cried inside to imagine what it was like for him to be so young and living so far away from family. I told myself that I didn't have options, so I needed to be grateful, though the more I told myself this, the more my chest hurt and my breath was constricted.

Taylor and I ran through the wide halls to Zachary's room, where we squatted down to squeeze Zachary until my legs hurt. Zachary had a superpower of being extremely in the moment and present with anyone willing to be in the moment with him. He was beaming. Time stood still, and I memorized this moment of the three of us being together. We packed up all of his equipment, medications, updated protocols, clothes, and diapers, and signed out of the facility. It was 15 degrees and dark, and the road back to our lodging in Massachusetts was long. But we were together. As we slowly unpacked Zachary's wheelchair from the car and unpacked all of our bags, I was nearly traumatized. In all my efforts to create a little Christmas spirit and our family reunion of three, I had forgotten Zachary's seizure medications. It was 11:30PM and still snowing outside. I prepared myself for the worst Christmas ever.

I woke the boys early the next morning; we were going to do something special since it was Christmas Day. We hopped in the car with our jammies on, and then went for a winter wonderland drive. Their job was to look for all the convenience stores that were open as we went through each of the little towns from Massachusetts back to New Hampshire. If they could find a store that was open, we would run in and each get any one snack we wanted. There was no limit; we could stop at every single store we found.

My head was full of voices about what kind of mother would spend Christmas day driving back to the facility to get seizure medication, and in the meantime, not even be exactly sure where all the nearby hospitals were in the probable event that Zachary would have a seizure I couldn't stop.

In the end, it was a Christmas miracle: no seizures. The day was one of literally being together, listening to a local radio station, and doing whatever we wanted to do that felt good. I had forgotten what it felt like be so present and flexible with each other that something real could unfold. I had forgotten that we could create any perspective that felt right to us, and even experiment with new ways to spend Christmas day together. I had lost track of those coaching skills that focused on listening beyond the words to what was available to us and important to us.

As the months passed, I worked hard to connect with each of the boys and then follow their lead. I had purchased a video camera so I could set up videoconferencing with Zachary at the institution. I recorded books on cassette tapes and mailed them to him to be played on the tape recorder by his bed.

Taylor had a cell phone, initially for safety reasons since he started to fly home solo, and also so we could have private conversations. Rather than me trying to dance around sticky topics or avoid stressful thoughts, I was invested in finding a way for Taylor to give voice to whatever was

going on with him. So, these conversations took different forms. "What is a metaphor for your life?" I asked him during one of our Sunday afternoon phone calls.

"What's a med-i-ford?"

"Well, it's a picture in your mind that describes what your life feels like."

"I dunno...."

"That's okay. If you **did** know, what kind of object would describe your life?"

"Nothing..." he paused. "If I have to pick a picture about my life I would say my life is like an ice cream cone. I thought it would be really, really good, except it melted all over and is a total mess, and I don't even want it."

"Yeah, sometimes ice cream is a total mess. That's a great mediford."
Boom.

Another way we would give voice to what was going on in our lives
was to describe any dreams we had. On one particular morning, we were
staying at a small respite apartment on campus and were sitting together
eating breakfast. I asked Taylor what his dream was about. He said he
didn't know, and I said that's a good place to start. I asked if he wanted to
draw it, and he silently picked up a scrap of paper. He drew some people
in a room with a low ceiling. He drew himself very tall and bending all
the way over so that he could fit in the room. His body looked like a giant
squeezing into a cramped single apartment room. He said, "In my dream
everything was too small, and I couldn't fit in." Boom.

This became our way of staying connected, without judging other people
and without being cut off from our own experiences. I don't remember
ever planning these kinds of conversations, and as I look back it sounds
more poetic than it actually felt. The pain of being apart both scared me
and scarred me. Over the years, I came to rely on one my strengths: spontaneously creating new ideas and new perspectives in a moment. This skill
could be over-used and become a weakness by not planning enough details
and relying on impromptu decision-making. As a long-distance parent,
however, I took risks to do whatever I could imagine to raise my two sons
to be all they could be and hold onto to our relationship by a thread.

CHAPTER 11

HARD WORK PAYS OFF

Taylor had started playing clarinet with his elementary-school band in Stratham, and their band was invited to perform at Disney World. I called to introduce myself to the band director and asked if I could chaperone. He graciously agreed, and I became one of eight parent chaperones. At the Orlando airport I reunited with Taylor and met the other three tweeners I would be chaperoning. I felt so happy to drop into a total moment of being a mom. I was in complete bliss with my roles and responsibilities as a chaperone. My formal duties were to provide direct supervision, though it was actually a chance to get to know Taylor's peers in his new life. It was a wonderful opportunity to watch and listen for what was top of mind for them and be available in any way I could to support them to have a memorable experience. We got rained on passing the yellow-backed Duiker and Okapi of the animal kingdom. I felt overwhelmed with emotion sitting in the back row for the George of the Jungle performance, which seemed to be all about a mother-son relationship. We ate ice cream and sprawled out on the concrete to dry after another rainstorm. The outdoor venue where Taylor's band performed had seats for 1800 people. If you counted the eight chaperones, there were only about 20 people who attended the concert. As the curtain opened, the students sat with their bodies perfectly erect in the 100% humidity in their black pants and long-sleeved white shirts. I wiped the tears away from my eyes ignoring anything going on the world outside of that precious moment.

The trip was one-part sweetness, one-part heartache, and one-part despair. I was able to finally be a mom again and do something I had long ago imagined in my hoped-for and dreamed-for family. It was also like tearing the scab off a deep wound, to have to say good-bye to Taylor, our small group, and the other moms and dads who got to live with their kids. Taylor and I had to say goodbye in the Orlando airport. Taylor draped his almost six-foot body on mine and found a soft smile to match the sparkle in his eyes. I wrapped my arms around him tightly and whispered the lines from a children story we'd read together.

"I love you from here to the moon and back, Taylor."

"I love you from here to the moon and back even more, mom."

I choked on my tears as people around us listened to MP3 players and chattered about the weather in New England. The mechanical, professional voice on the overhead system called for someone to go to the nearest courtesy phone. Luckily it wasn't for me.

I had lost any sense of direction in my own life. Again. I couldn't be honest about my own opinions about raising a child with a disability at home in an ordinary community because I felt like I was living a lie. I had already given up hope for my "dreamed of" fantasy family after Zachary's diagnosis, then again after my divorce. Now however, I was living a lie of even being a mother.

While I strangled myself with these repeated thoughts, there were three conversations that crossed my path through three different people. I can remember each specific moment and recall exactly how each of them said something to me that I couldn't understand, though given the absence of any other lifeline, I grabbed what they offered.

The first occurred when my friend Julie drove over in her large black Suburban soon after the boys had moved away. She knocked as she opened the door and walked right in. I was sitting at the kitchen table, feeling like that skeleton who walked into a bar looking for a drink and a mop—empty and invisible.

"How are you?"

"I don't know. I just don't know."

"Sandy, I am worried about you. You need to find something to do so you don't collapse into Mike. You cannot make him the center of your world. You need to get committed to something—a job or something else."

Our home was still; our yard was quiet. I couldn't hear the kids across the street playing in the neighborhood pool, and I couldn't hear what Julie was saying. I was so hurt. Julie adored Mike. Julie had children with disabilities. I could usually count on her to get how difficult my life was. I practiced my Sears-clerk mantra and said, "Thank you so very much," and she left.

The second conversation happened in a bar. Mike had asked me to dinner at the Jefferson Street Grill.

"I can't find my next step in terms of what to do professionally." I was still working full-time for the CDE as Director of The Coaching Project and consulting as a coach with a national training company, though I had an urge to do something more. I dipped my French fry in the ketchup, and Mike ordered two more gin and tonics. The back of my thighs were sticking to the red vinyl bar stool.

"What else do you really want to do?"

"I feel silly telling you this. When I was in high school, I ordered *Entrepreneur* magazine because I wanted to own my own business."

"You own Sandy Scott & Associates. Go ahead and expand." Mike had a conviction in his voice, and I heard it.

My heart skipped a beat. My gremlins were caught completely off guard and had nothing to say. There was something exciting about getting serious and expanding my work. I had been feeling over my head and worried that people would sniff me out as someone living an incongruent life, though I also really, really, wanted to get out in front of my life and never feel like this again. I wanted to get off this rollercoaster of feeling like my life was just getting started and then collapsing. It was at that moment, I invested in expanding Sandy Scott & Associates.

The third person who crossed my path was Dr. Corry Robinson, Professor of Pediatrics and Psychiatry at University of Colorado School of Medicine. She was very influential across the state of CO, and she was a member of the Colorado Interagency Coordinating Council. Corry provided leadership, direction to interdisciplinary professional staff to more than forty faculty members, and had been Principal Investigator on more than 30 federally funded research projects in the field of developmental and intellectual disabilities. She was uber-smart and very intimidating.

The grant for the next year of The Coaching Project was going to be moved to Corry's organization, and she wanted to have lunch. I had come to terms with fear and failure and couldn't wait to get this lunch over with, in part because I couldn't think of a single topic about which I could feel smart enough to talk. That being said, I was smart enough to show up to lunch and not cancel just because I was a chicken.

We met in Corry's office. She was entirely approachable and kind. In fact, she was the introvert, and I was the extrovert. She started by asking if I had ever considered getting my Ph.D. I grew silent. I suddenly became an instant introvert. I was running through a quick flow chart of possible responses.

I could say "No," and then tell her my GPA from under-graduate work was borderline embarrassing.

I could say "No," and then tell her she does not know me very well. I am not smart enough.

I could say "No," and then inform her that this whole lunch is one big mistake.

Or I could say. "Nope."

I said, "Nope."

She packed her small briefcase, and we walked a block to a deli. She quietly planted some seeds while I hardly said a word. She told me that my title with the new grant would change to be aligned with the School of Medicine, and I could go to school for my master's degree if I wanted to. All expense would be paid through this new grant.

By the time we got back to her office, I found some of my words. "What program requires the fewest credits to graduate and could be relevant to my personal convictions?" I had to admit, if I was only going to speak a few words, this was a good start.

Corry opened the University of Colorado Graduate School catalog and showed me some options. She said I would need to ask three people for letters of recommendation and submit an application. Quickly. The deadline for enrollment was right around the corner.

I didn't stop to think about any of this. I drove home and sent letters to people I had met who had been influential and personally impacted my life. To this day, I have a binder with 23 letters inside. The first letter is from the Dean of University of Colorado at Denver's Graduate School of Public Affairs. The letter acknowledged The Graduate School of Public Affairs was "one of the outstanding schools of public administration in the country. The *US News and World Report*'s most recent survey placed GSPA in the top 15% of schools of public administration throughout the nation." The next invited me to schedule an appointment to discuss the Accelerated MPA option. The third letter congratulated me for acceptance into the Executive MPA program I could complete in less than two years while working full-time.

The other 20 letters were from the people who actually wrote a letter to champion something in me that I seriously could **not** see. I organized them into a portfolio, and I left that book by my bedside for many years. I will never forget what can happen when we stop to see each other and believe in each other, especially when we can't possibly see ourselves.

The years that followed were an intense time of school, work, and long-distance parenting. I didn't have much space for friends, sleeping, or breathing unless the boys and I were together. I continued to have breathing problems, though it would often happen when no one was watching, so I ignored it myself.

In my graduate program, I ended each course with a final exam and created a one-page document with the best tools, model, or tips I wanted to lock in and remember. I learned best by bottom-lining my key takeaways from each class, and I loved building my own little set of Cliff's notes related to public administration. In my career, I expanded my coaching work. I coached executives in Asia, Europe, the Pacific Rim, and across the U.S. I coached senior executives in finance, education, telecommunications, and business. I coached them as people first, rather than by their label or role and noticed that as I brought more of me to the conversation, it was an invitation for each person to bring more of themselves. I had learned the impact of bringing our full selves way back at Zachary's first IFSP meeting, when physicians spoke as whole humans and not just as doctors.

I felt the shame inside of me convert into fierceness. I was trying to monitor my own inner dialogue so I could update my own perceptions of my life, my family, and my world-view. I wondered how I could forgive everyone who had impacted my life in a way that took me off track from the life I expected. How could I go about cultivating an attitude of acting as if our family was going to be okay, when my heart was still full of doubt? How could I weave these fragile new insights into my own life's purpose?

I didn't know how, so I just kept working.

I was on track to complete my master's degree in 1.5 years. I had maintained a GPA above 3.5, submitted two research papers, and chosen a colleague, Stacey, to co-write a master's thesis. Stacey and I had similar passions and different strengths. She was very detailed oriented and systematic in her processes. I had experience in working with someone who had similar passions and different strengths, and felt a lot of synergy so I figured this would be a stroll in the park.

After we reviewed the very prescribed process and detailed procedures required to just *prepare* to *submit* our thesis proposal in *accordance with the Guidelines,* I was bushed. I think it would have been easier to take a hike with Zachary on a rocky mountain trail uphill in the dark both ways than engage in the first step of this process.

But we did it. We consulted with faculty advisors, selected our thesis committee, and developed a concise problem statement we wanted to investigate. We established a research hypothesis related to exploring a more systematic way to unleash leadership potential in the realm of Part C IDEA public policy. We dug down deep to find books, journals, and resources, and then designed and implemented an interview methodology to gather new data. We analyzed the data, wrote some recommendations, and eventually went before our committee to present.

The process was grueling, especially since we were both working full-time. I learned a lot about myself during the process. Actually, I didn't learn about myself; my partner, Stacey would graciously observe things about me and then diplomatically articulate something that I couldn't deny.

"Where do you want to meet to start compiling the data?" Stacey was focused.

"Let's meet at our home in Bellvue this Thursday at 4PM. We can organize all the data on post-it notes and then wallpaper the boys' room."

"I'm fine to meet at your home, though we will probably need a different method to examine the data in more depth." Stacey was a natural fact finder and had an innate way of quantifying subjective data, ranking ordering particulars of any project and removing ambiguity so that any topic could be defined in terms of exactitude.

I was dog-tired and really just wanted to get the damn thing done. Stacey agreed to try the wall-paper-post-it approach. By day three, Mike walked in the room and had an observation. "Hi, ladies."

"Hi." The color-coded post-its were falling off the wall.

"What the heck are you doing?" Stacey glanced at me and quickly looked back at her notes.

I glanced around the room wondering why this was becoming so complicated.

"Sandy had this creative idea about how to organize the data from our research by writing key phrases from our phone interviews on post-its and then organizing them by themes on all the walls." Stacey made the process sound more rationale than it really was.

"You gotta be kidding me. Why aren't you ladies using Excel to compile and analyze your data?" Mike looked completely stumped.

Under stress or task saturation, I ignored my mistakes and would take risks without considering the consequences. In times like this, I acted like rules were boring and unnecessary. Under stress, I tended to be uber flexible, spontaneous, and—gulp—impulsive. When all was right with the world, I could manage these tendencies and work well with others. It was just in times of extreme pressure, like getting the damn thesis done, that these behaviors reared their nasty heads. I needed to continue to cultivate my own internal landscape of ways to develop myself and my career. It became important for me to acknowledge my mistakes rather than finesse my way out of them, adhere to important rules more consistently, and renegotiate commitments rather than ignore them, and update plans.

I think Stacey may have wondered about my reliability toward the end of this process. On our appointed day to defend our thesis to our committee in Denver, we were huddled in the car, finalizing our talking points and making sure we had followed all instructions in copying and binding our thesis for distribution. Fortunately, we had interacted with all of the committee members ahead of time and had practiced presenting how the research was conducted, the measurements we used, and our conclusions. Once we got past the initial anxiety of feeling like we were standing in front of an execution squad, we were focused and confident.

I graduated in May 2004 with my degree in the Executive Master's Public Administration program through University of Colorado's Graduate School of Public Policy. It was bittersweet. My family, including Mike and my grandma, watched me walk across the stage to get my diploma. I couldn't find a way to fly my kids to the ceremony, so a part of me felt incomplete. I took a breath and then started looking for a full-time position with healthcare benefits.

I sent out application after application for three weeks and was painfully aware I was not getting any interviews. It was exhausting. Some days felt hopeless. A friend recommended I reach out to a friend of a colleague who suggested I call a woman named Pat. Pat took my phone call and was a breath of fresh air. She described a Service Excellence position at a healthcare system, and I liked the sound of it. Actually I couldn't believe a position like this existed—it sounded too good to be true. The job description focused on developing and leading the staff to bring quality care and excellence to each patient experience. The vision was to ensure each patient would enter and leave the facility with a positive health outcome and then would recommend the hospital to others. In my mind this was a series of individual, group, and organizational coaching engagements. The job sounded like a great way to use coaching skills to engage staff and physicians to enjoy their work and in doing so, to ensure patients had positive experiences.

I interviewed in the conference center of the hospital, was offered the position, and told to begin July 4th, 2004. I left our family reunion at Spirit Lake early for my first day of work.

I worked long hours in my new role. As I collaborated with teams across the hospital, I was shocked that I could leverage my experience raising Zachary in a new way. I talked about the impact of sitting beside a patient at eye-level or lower and how to face heart-to-heart with each other when speaking. In my first hospital role, I began to notice how leadership for me was about living and leading more fully. I began to share parts of my own journey as Zachary's mom. I described my own sense of what happens when we listen to each other and to our patients more fully.

A new Chief Executive Officer was hired. He exuded confidence and had a vision of being a top performing hospital with a focus on five areas: Employee engagement, patient satisfaction, quality, physician friendly, and finances. He reorganized the leadership team. As part of the reorganization, I now reported directly to him, and I became a member of the administrative council (AC). One of the responsibilities of being on AC was to carry the pager on a rotating schedule. The person with the pager was the designated leader to be on call for the entire hospital for that particular weekend. I was shocked that I could be trained to do this, and I felt huge responsibility to do my job well. Another responsibility of being on AC was to meet every other week. The agenda focused on reviewing data, sharing best practices, and committing to next steps ensuring we would achieve top-decimal performance as the leadership team of the hospital.

On June 14th, 2005 our CEO came into my office and closed the door. He didn't do this often, so he had my full attention. Our performance for patient satisfaction had started to decline. The scary part was that members of the administrative council who missed the target for 90 days would be removed from their role. The good news was that the CEO was fully supportive of whatever we leaders needed so the hospital would consistently hit the targets.

My office was 12 feet by 12 feet. The hard cushion made noise when the CEO sat down; his back was against the full-length windows looking right at me.

"The patient-satisfaction scores are not acceptable."

I had been coming in to work earlier and earlier each morning and feeling worried. "I don't know what to do."

"Yes, you do. Go back to the basics."

"Ok, I'll start working on a plan." I felt relieved that I could take time to do research and gather some new ideas about how to re-engage the staff. My shoulders relaxed, and I could feel myself breathe again.

"I will call a Code Orange across the hospital PA system, a signal of an internal disaster at 10AM."

My throat made a loud noise as I swallowed. My eyes darted at the clock. It was 7:35AM.

"What's going to happen after that?"

"You will address the hospital leadership team with confidence about how to go back to the basics of whatever it is that you've taught them in the past." My mind darted around; my eyes looked for a solution in mid-air. "Do you have any questions?"

It felt like career suicide, though I wondered if this was a practical joke or some kind of male humor that I was missing. "Are you serious about this?"

"Yes."

"Then I think you need to leave so I can find my confidence."

I focused. I gathered materials about going back to the basics of what we as a team needed to do. I put together a simple power point, got still, and listened for the code orange alarm at 10AM.

That day I learned a little bit more about how to be authentic and trust there were things that I did know that I didn't even know I knew. I trusted he had my back. The code orange alert went off as promised. Leaders from across the hospital came to the boardroom. The CEO waited until all leaders were present and then announced the internal disaster. Our patient-satisfaction scores were below goal and beginning to decline.

He did not say much, though his message was clear; then I did my 20-minute presentation. I focused on going back to the basics of what matters to patients.

Later that year, the hospital won "Best of the Best" of the entire hospital system. In fact, the hospital won the award the next six out of seven years.

The CEO rounded the entire hospital daily. One afternoon he came to my office to discuss the hospital team's performance. Before he left he asked if there was anything else I wanted him to know. I felt terribly awkward, but I seized the moment: "I wonder if the hospital would pay for me to take the Board of Governor's exam through the American College of Healthcare Executives." I knew this was one of the credentials for anyone interested in an executive role in hospital administration.

"Sure—why not?"

"Well, the previous CEO said that I didn't qualify."

"Yes, you do. Go register. By passing the exam, you will be a Fellow of the AHCE. What date do you want to be Board Certified in Healthcare Management?"

"Uh…. I'll get back to you." I wondered if he was kidding. He wasn't kidding. "Thank you. Thank you very much." And he walked out.

Within moments, I hopped online and ordered a bunch of books. I studied at night. I studied a lot. I did not take any short-cuts. I did not ignore my mistakes, and I followed a rigorous study plan. I was nervous, though I felt ready, so I scheduled the exam. I arrived at the strip mall in Cheyenne, Wyoming, to take the designated computer-based test, which was timed. The final question asked, "Did you complete the test?" I clicked the yes button. The little hourglass on the screen rotated clockwise and then stopped. I opened the electronic envelope with my results. I'd failed the test by one damn question.

I was so angry that I had sacrificed spending time with Mike, given up workouts at the gym, and put my relationships with girlfriends on hold. I had been diligent about reading, compiling study notes, and whatever the heck intelligent fact-finding people do.

I decided I was not going to sacrifice another chunk of my life. I decided not to take the exam again.

Then, one September afternoon, on the eve of the autumn solstice, I was driving up Big Thompson Canyon to meet some women for an overnight retreat in Estes Park. I still felt irritated I had failed the exam. I decided to make a deal. I set aside all the voices in my head and in a screaming, silent prayer said, "Okay—here is The Deal. If I get a clear and direct sign by the time I get home tomorrow that I should take the ACHE exam, then I will take it again. No more questions. If I do not get a clear and direct sign by the time I get home tomorrow, then I will not take the exam, and I will not have this conversation again. Do I make myself clear?"

At this point, I was building my own muscle of listening beyond the words, establishing trust through honesty and sincerity, and being increasingly present and flexible during conversations. I learned how to "dance in the moment" with individual and group conversations, and access my own intuition. I even learned from my master coach training how to "listen for what is trying to be said—even if it means being silent and allowing it to be said through others."

So, this screaming Deal was a bit on the edge of trusting my inner knowing. I had this strong sense of how I could chart my future career by being board certified in both healthcare management and coaching. I had a gut feeling that I just needed to find a way to put this failure to rest.

The drive up to the condo we were sharing in Estes Park was about 32 miles along the Big Thompson River, which ran parallel to the Cache la Poudre River. Somewhere after my big fit of angst, I passed a small rustic resort—the Cache la Poudre Cabins. I had never noticed it before. The beat-up, weathered cabins were easy to drive by and ignore. Except today. The neon sign was blinking. The "C" of Cache was burnt out completely, while the "ache" of Cache was brightly lit. I read it as "ACHE."

I registered for the Board of Governor's Exam again. I reviewed the books and met with colleagues who were subject-matter experts in the field of hospital administration. I took time to really learn more about the 10 core knowledge areas. The areas were: Governance & Organizational Structure, Human Resources, Finance, Healthcare Technology & Information Management, Quality & Performance Improvement, Laws & Regulations, Professionalism & Ethics, Healthcare, Management & Business. I passed the test, and I learned how afraid I was to fail, and how powerless I felt in that moment of failure. I learned how to ask for help and work harder.

Now that I had a career-track with healthcare benefits, a predictable paycheck, and the opportunity to work with teams in a healthcare environment, I felt 50% complete. If I could only find a way to eliminate long-distance parenting and be part of a cohesive and healing family.

The summer of 2005 Taylor was 12 years old and wore a size 10.5 men's sneaker. He spent the summer with Mike and me in Bellvue and re-established relationships with some elementary-school friends. They watched movies from the back of the pickup truck at our local Drive-In theatre. He rode his 80 cc dirt bike across the 16 acres of pasture where we lived and named parts of the trail. On the far north end of pasture, the trail made a sharp hairpin turn to the left and dropped about six feet into a steep ravine. Taylor called it "Suicide Curve." Taylor saved his allowance money that he earned that summer and bought his own Crossman 1077 pellet gun. Mike and I bought our first used kayak, and the three of us paddled around Horsetooth Reservoir just 150 yards from our home. We spent most of our free time together outside doing chores, grilling burgers, and shooting pellet guns at pop cans on the rocks. I splurged one afternoon and rented a jet ski for Taylor and me. We spent two hours on the reservoir practicing the same moves we'd watched in the James Bond movie, *The Spy Who Loved Me.*

Mike, Taylor, and I went back to our annual family reunion at Spirit Lake. As a little boy, Taylor used to call it "Spirit Yakes." We played board games and card games on the porch with our cousins and sat on the boat dock in front of our cabin. There was always a part of these trips that felt nostalgic and centering to me. Each year we took photos of cousins on the porch swing, and this year in particular, all the male cousins, including Mike and Taylor, huddled around the swing. On the one hand, I felt like my life was becoming whole again. On the other hand, I felt a great big emptiness in my chest, especially when we took the boat to the middle of the lake to drop an anchor and swim. I missed Zachary terribly. The worst part was that I couldn't tell if I was missing the boy he was or the boy I wanted him to be. He loved the water and loved spending time on the porch. Zachary loved the low-key, "lake-time" vibe of these visits, though it was getting increasingly harder for me to transport him back and support all of his needs. I used to bring Zachary to the lakes when he was younger. Now, though, the thought of packing all of his equipment, flying to Massachusetts, driving to the institution in New Hampshire, driving back to the airport, flying to Iowa, driving to Spirit Lake, supporting all of his needs without a childcare provider, and then flying back again sounded like a logistical nightmare. I felt like I wasn't doing enough for my kids—and like I was abandoning Zachary even more. Was I really trying hard enough? I felt a guilt I wasn't sure would ever go away.

During the summer, Taylor and I hiked the high mountain trails of Colorado's Routt National Forest Steamboat Springs. Sometimes he brought a friend, and sometimes we hiked with a small group of parent/tweener friends. One of our hikes started at the base of Cameron Pass, elevation

10,276. The thing I did right on this trip was pack enough water. The thing I did wrong was not keep track of where we were going. I was caught up in the rapture of the fields of wildflowers and lost my bearings. We made it to the summit and got a lot of great photos, though we got lost coming down and couldn't find our car. We were exhausted, and Taylor turned into an open book. We eventually found our car but not before I had learned all about the first girl Taylor kissed.

The next trail we hiked was up Steamboat Mountain. We could see the summit right in front of us like it was a stone's throw away. I was real clear on which trails we could take up to the top. I got maps, I marked them, and was not going to make that mistake again. Unfortunately, I was not as prepared in packing water, and we had a close call of a different kind on that day.

While Taylor and I lived with Mike in Bellvue, I had started renting 1808 Centennial Road. I posted an ad in the paper and met a young student, Amos, who was hard working, though shy on cash. I had never rented property before, though I knew what it was like to have someone believe in you when you doubted yourself. The new tenant and I made an agreement on the monthly rent. We agreed he would pay 80% of my mortgage payment and leverage his passion of fixing things. He wanted to attend Colorado State University and get a degree in construction, so we made a plan. He maintained the inside and outside of the home, and I paid for the materials for him to do small repairs as needed. Taylor assisted the young student in hosting a garage sale to get rid of stuff in the condo we didn't want anymore. Our tenant ended up splitting the cash from the garage sale with Taylor, and they each walked away with $119.50.

Mike's home just outside Fort Collins had three small bedrooms, so we went ahead and remodeled one of the bedrooms to be Taylor's and one to be Zachary's. Taylor squeezed the drum set we'd given him the year before into his room, and we set up Zachary's room with posters and board games. We learned a lot about how to communicate and of failures to communicate. Taylor was concrete and random. Mike was concrete and sequential. I was abstract and random. We were forging new frontiers as a wobbly new family.

By winter of 2005, I had flown to New Hampshire nine times, and one or both of the boys had flown to Colorado three times. After four years of the boys living in NH, things not going very well for Taylor in his blended family, Jonathan asked me if Taylor could move back to Colorado to live with me. I jumped on it in a heartbeat. I knew I had the capacity to do that, though I was still unable to figure out how to parent Zachary 100% full-time and work without any support.

The stress at Jonathan's house was high, and things were spiraling downwards quickly. Taylor described his life like being on a boat and all of his attention was on battening down the hatches. Someone else was in charge of the boat, and ever since he'd left Colorado, he felt like he was on a ship sailing straight into a storm—dark, unsafe, and without control of his own life.

By the time Taylor flew to Colorado for Christmas of 2005, I had met with the principal of the local junior high in LaPorte, the small town next to where Mike and I were living. The principal and his team were very welcoming, and together the school staff and I made a transition plan for Taylor to transfer to his new school. Everything was quickly set up. Jonathan and I agreed not to tell Taylor until after Christmas break, and I was working very hard to present a unified front with him. Taylor flew back to New Hampshire after Christmas break. When he landed at the Manchester airport, Jonathan called to say Taylor had arrived safely. He also said that he'd changed his mind and would not be sending Taylor back.

Click.

End of conversation.

Those four years of co-parenting were some of the most painful years of my life. Part of the pain was the distinct awareness that co-parenting was a total catastrophe and that the boys were showing signs of distress. There seemed to be a deep sense of mistrust on Jonathan's part; I felt extreme social withdrawal when we met in the parking lot to pick up or drop off Taylor. I felt like I was walking on eggshells because I didn't know what kind of mood Jonathan would be in. I just wanted us to get along. I didn't want anyone to feel a sense of criticism or worry about mistakes. Prior to the boys moving to NH, there was conflict about medical appointments. There was conflict if I called to tell Jonathan that Zachary had 15 seizures in 24 hours, and there was conflict if didn't tell him Zachary had 15 seizures in 24 hours and instead scheduled a neurology appointment to get his medications adjusted. In fact, while Jonathan was living in CO, he filed a motion with his attorney seeking to hold me in contempt of court for multiple items like this. The whole situation grew worse. Everything I read said it was critical to present a united front to the kids. I was focused on not undermining or impairing Zachary or Taylor's fragile relationships in their New Hampshire family, yet I felt like a fraud to not acknowledge what seemed pretty obvious. There was no space to come together and focus on what was in the "best interest of the children."

The following spring, I received a very unexpected phone call from Jonathan.

"Pamela, the four kids, and I are moving back to Colorado."

My eyes burst wide open, and I ran my fingers through my hair. "Are you serious?" I started to weep, and time stood still.

"We are moving back at the end of next month when school gets out."

I wanted to say something like "Holy hell," though I was scrambling to find better words.

"Jonathan, is this for real this time?"

The conversation was short and the follow-up emails loaded with surprises. Jonathan insisted on maintaining nearly 100 percent custody, with one overnight during the weekend. He asked if he, Zachary, and Taylor could live at 1808 Centennial Road during the weekdays. His plan was to buy a home for Pamela and their two daughters in Fort Collins; he acknowledged that it was not working for Pamela to live with the boys.

I quickly made arrangements for the college student to end the lease. I cleaned the condo so that Zachary, Taylor, and Jonathan could move. I would continue to live in Bellvue during the weekdays, and then I would live at the condo on the weekends with the boys. Jonathan would live there during the weekdays and then go live with his wife and two daughters a few miles away in a new home he bought for them on the weekends. Zachary and Taylor could stop moving (Taylor had moved three times in four years, and Zachary had moved four times in four years) and belong to a family among the friends, family, neighborhood, church, and physicians who knew them and loved them.

Mike was thrilled Zachary and Taylor would be moving back. He was cautious, though, saying the plan did not really make sense. He said it didn't make sense that a husband would not be living full time with his wife. He said something didn't seem right. I didn't care.

I agreed to the plan Jonathan proposed. Zachary, Taylor, and Jonathan moved into Centennial Road the summer of 2006.

PART IV

Zachary and I looking for wild iris in our CO pasture

Taylor and I hiking our annual 14,000-ft. mountain together.

CHAPTER 12

ONE STEP FORWARD, TWO STEPS BACK

I can describe Zachary in two very different ways. This forces me to notice the power of perspective. One way to describe him would be to list the medications he takes daily.

1. Lacosamide — seizure management
2. Clobazam — seizure management
3. Levetiracetam — seizure management
4. Hydrocodone-acetaminophen — hip pain
5. Coumadin — manage blood clots
6. Acetaminophen — manage hip pain
7. Ibuprofen — manage hip pain
8. Carafate — treats ulcers and stomach problems
9. Glucosamine-chondroitin — reduce joint pain
10. Prevacid — treats gastroesophageal reflux

11. Claritin   manage allergies

12. Miralax   stool softener

13. Benzocaine   manage acne

14. Retin-a gel   manage acne

15. Boost Plus   nutrition

16. Multi-vitamin   nutrition

17. Robinul   reduce drooling

18. Cerave moisturizer   skin care

19. Cetaphil   skin care

In addition, Zachary has an extremely outstretched bladder, so he is catheterized twice a day and is given fluids via his gastrostomy tube (G-tube) twice daily.

His wheel chair weighs about 185 pounds dry and needs constant attention. The upholstery of the seat needs to be soaked with cleaners frequently to eliminate the odor of urine, and replacement parts take forever to get in the mail.

Coordinating medical appointments is a part-time job, much like running a family-owned business. Each appointment focuses on different issues, yet often asks the same information. It seems like it would be easy to organize all of the medical reports, lab results, doctor recommendations, resources, and care plans, though it's like learning multiple different languages and often saying one thing when you mean another, or hearing one thing and misunderstanding the main point.

Zachary's visits to the hospital have increased in frequency and duration as he has grown. They started with simple visits to the ER to manage his seizures, and now are becoming more complex with osteomyelitis, esophageal varices, blood clots in his heart, extreme hip displacement/pain, complex partial seizures, generalized seizures, absence seizures, myoclonic seizures, tonic and clonic seizures, grand mal seizures, atonic seizures, and partial seizures.

And yet, there is another way to describe Zachary: As a baby, he and I took long walks along the country road between our house and the lumber mill just down the road. He took baths in the kitchen sink, in part because we had a tall counter, and as a 6' mom, this was delightful. He wore the same baptism dress as his great grandfather, grandfather, and me, his mother, and by age three was on the front page of *Colorado Parent* magazine promoting outdoor adventures with his family.

Zachary attended a local morning preschool filled with science activities like "carrots and beets," social studies activities like "My Neighborhood," math activities like "One, Two, Buckle My Shoe," reading time, naps, and snacks. We walked to school together, where he attended our local full-day kindergarten. As a family, we've skied, run 5K races on holidays, and ridden bicycles along the bike paths of Fort Collins. We traveled a lot with a focus on visiting the National Parks like Yellowstone, Rocky Mountain National Park, Niagara Falls, and even the free whooping crane viewing decks of Kearney, Nebraska.

I tell myself that Zachary attended a private residency school for three years (otherwise known as an institution for severely handicapped kids). Otherwise, he attended the local elementary school, then junior high, and high school. He swam at the neighborhood pool in the summer, sold popcorn at the football games with high school friends, and worked out at the Raintree Health Club gym, where we had a family membership for 15 years. Later, he got into watching college football with Mike and went to the local pub Thursday nights to do whatever guys do during football season. We had two dogs and lots of chores around the house. Zachary's an easy-going guy who flirted with girls and observed the mischief of his younger brother, Taylor.

So, there you have it. One son, two truths.

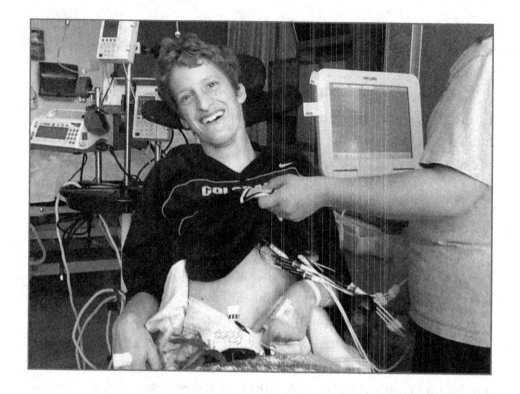

As a coach, I know people can build the muscle to observe what is going on in our lives—almost like watching ourselves through a video camera. We can build the muscle of noticing what is going on and then choose any perspective that we want. Perspective is one of the gifts we can give each other, especially when everything is falling apart or it feels like there is no way forward. Sometimes a person can show up to meet us where we are and be with us as we find our way.

In 2006, with the boys back in Colorado, I was invested in establishing a fresh start for our blended family. I looked for things we could do together: A step-dad who liked to ride horses, though not walk, two teen-age boys struggling to find their place among two blended families, and a mom with a vision of spending time together.

With this in mind, I signed Mike, Taylor, and me up for the 2006 Horsetooth Half Marathon race. It was a bad idea, a miserable race, and a good example of how I tend to act under stress. I didn't ask for my family's input; I was unrealistically optimistic. On the morning of the race it felt like the beginning of another Cold War. Mike was quiet and distant. Taylor sat in the back of the cargo van on the floor listening to his iPod. I looked at Zachary for a lifeline of hope, and he smiled ear to ear.

We slowly climbed out of the 1987 brown Ford van and silently pinned our race bibs on ourselves. I put on my happy face and chatted non-stop about the upcoming event. "What a great morning to do this together as a family!"

Mike ignored my comments and got Zachary's seizure medications, diaper, and race bib. Taylor kicked a rock in the dirt parking lot and said nothing. "It might look steep, but we can do anything if we do it together!" I was determined to remain upbeat.

We dragged ourselves to the tail end of the startup line, and the Cold War turned into the Ice Age. Mike stared at the ground, his only focus to get to the finish line with least amount of pain (afterwards was told by his doctor he needed a total hip replacement because he was bone on bone.) Taylor didn't want to be around the tension, so each time we approached a steep hill, he lagged further and further behind. Zachary fell asleep in the jogger, and I told myself everything was going to be okay. The race started with a 6.4% incline, followed by a 9.2% incline, a few more steep hills, followed by a run along the east side of Horsetooth Reservoir and then a long flat path beside the Poudre River trail.

As long as we were doing something together—even if tensions were high—I could quiet the gremlins in my head. If I stopped for a moment, the gremlins would scream: "You are not even a real family! You are a group of misfits and don't even look like you belong together. No wonder others see you as a defective family; you cannot even get along on a simple walk."

Disappointment washed over me for a blink, and then I immediately ignored my feelings. I was scared to death if I let myself feel ashamed or show my desperation, I would enter a lifetime of depression and never come up for air again. We didn't train for the event. We just did it. In my desperate need to find our way to work through my fears and be a family, I tried to persuade everyone to just be happy. It never occurred to me to tell the truth about how scared I felt in re-establishing ourselves as a blended family. It never occurred to me that it could be healthy to talk about sad feelings together and then work together to re-write our future.

The following year when the same race came around, I had a different idea. I asked Mike and Taylor to meet Zachary and me at the finish line. I then went scouting for a child-care provider who had experience running marathons. It would be Zachary's 17th birthday coming up, and it seemed to me that most guys Zachary's age were into speed and girls. If Zachary could participate in the half marathon, just once, he could get a bit of both. And I could check off that he was experiencing "normal" life as a 17-year-old.

I had heard about a girl named Kelly Van Denend, who was providing support for another young man with multiple disabilities. She was a student at Colorado State University in the Occupational Therapy department and looking for additional hours to work. Kelly was a woman of intoxicating compassion who was up for the challenge. She and Zachary trained a bit, largely by running a few miles with Zachary in an adult jogger along the hills of the reservoir. The week before the race, I decided to join them, so I went to the gym to work out on the elliptical machine for 30 minutes daily. Then I called the race director to ask if we could start an hour early so we didn't come in last place. In my heart, this was all about supporting Zachary to be the "speed, girls, party atmosphere" of a fun race, not coming in last place at sunset when they are packing up the porta pottys and everyone is gone. Again. The race director gladly agreed to let us begin early.

The morning of the race, Kelly, Zachary, and I put on our race bands. We had Zachary's seizure drugs and magnet to swipe over his VNS if he had seizures while on the course. The VNS (Vagus Nerve Stimulation) is a device used to treat epilepsy, especially for people who continue to have seizures while on seizure medications. It involves implanting the device under the skin lying over the left upper chest, as it is the left vagus nerve that receives nerve input and relays it to the brain. A hand-held programming wand looking like an iPhone is used by a neurologist to direct the implanted device to send electric pulses at regular intervals up the left vagus nerve to the brain. One of the purposes is to prevent seizure activity. If a seizure does begin, though, we just swiped a special magnet over his chest where the device is implanted, lightly stroking the skin with the magnet. This would send additional impulses to the person's brain to stop or reduce the seizure activity.

As we started up the first big hill, Kelly pushed Zachary to the top. As we approached the next, Kelly pushed Zachary to the top again. Zachary was smiling. He always got the giggles in yoga classes when people exhaled together, and now he got to listen to Kelly and me sucking in air and exhaling with robust sound effects. Kelly and Zachary jogged the entire course along Horsetooth Reservoir. The reservoir sits in the foothills above the town to the west side of the Dakota Hogback red mountains. The reservoir runs north-south for seven miles and is a mecca for people who like to boat, swim, paddleboard, hike, climb, camp out, or just picnic. We watched the early morning rowers pull in unison along the west side of the reservoir. A couple on mountain bikes were riding the dirt trail below us near the shoreline. Above, I could see a giant bird hovering above us. I was toggling between sheer euphoria because Zachary was loving the outdoor experience and fighting with the voices in my head saying "I can't believe I made Mike, with a painful hip, and Taylor, a teenager, do this with me... this course is ridiculously difficult..."

By the time we got to the flat path along the river, something happened that I still don't know how to explain. After speed walking all the hills, my body suddenly cramped up along the innocent concrete slab of a trail. I couldn't put one foot in front of the other. Kelly assisted me, and Zachary sat and smiled. We started to move forward along the trail again as people passed us. I wanted to stop people and try to explain that I wasn't a complete wimp. Perhaps karma was catching up with me from the year before. God seemed to have noticed.

The final part of the trail was a mile from the finish line, and when we crossed over the line, a man approached us. He had a twinkle in his eye, the jolly spirit of Santa Claus, though athletic, having about .25 ounces of extra weight on him if you counted his sweaty shift. He said a few words and then got a bit choked up and asked if he could do a race with Zachary someday. I know that I tried to use my most polite words, though the only thing that came out of my mouth was, "Where have you been?" I personally vowed to never run a half-marathon again. I was in total pain.

We exchanged phone numbers, and fortunately he wrote down his name.

I increasingly became aware of something about myself. When I feel seen or heard, or when I sense that someone can see or hear others, I immediately trust that person. In fact, I may trust that person more than they trust themselves. I can see possibilities that others didn't see. This is not a fuzzy feeling; this is a very practical, no-nonsense awareness I have. It's not a belief. It is a knowing.

I had a knowing about this guy, and his name was Dennis Vanderheiden.

Little did I know that Dennis was an Ironman triathlete who had a vision of partnering with a person who had a disability to compete in races.

Dennis came to our home the next week to meet Zachary. They developed a very real relationship and went on to launch a non-profit, Athletes in Tandem. AiT became a non-profit organization of athletes competing in cycling, running & triathalon events. Dennis had a vision of how people of all abilities could increase their quality of life thru an active lifestyle and become a part of the community of outdoor enthusiasts. Over the next five years, Zachary would complete 45 races, including 12 triathalons and a series of other running/long-distance swim races.

ColoradO2 Photography ©

In 2007 I felt restless. I wondered how to deepen the coaching mindset, coaching skills, and the coaching "way of being" into the fabric of more people more quickly. I was feeling driven, though my own coaching was plateauing. I could feel it, though I didn't take time to do much about it. Actually, I didn't take much time to do anything outside of work and meeting with my lawyer to discuss custody issues, supporting the boys to readjust to their move back to Colorado, and staying connected with Zachary's medical teams.

Ever since the boys had moved back, I'd requested 50/50 custody of Taylor. I had 50% custody of Zachary, though only visitation with Taylor on weekends. My attorney said that since I had released custody of the boys in 2002, their dad did not need to share custody with me. I was completely blindsided by this and struggled again with the decision I had made back then. I worried about Taylor. I worried that he was navigating complex family dynamics on top of junior high school peer pressures. I could feel the unspoken conversations that needed to happen. I didn't want Taylor to absorb any of my fears and concerns, so I danced a silent dance with Jonathan to find time to connect with Taylor. I negotiated time so that I could take Taylor to confirmation class at Plymouth Congregational Church on Wednesday nights, where he'd been baptized. Wednesday nights were my favorite night of the week. I would pick Taylor up at the end of the road from where he now lived at his dad's house and drive 10 mph below the speed limit all the way down Horsetooth Ave. I worked hard to have casual conversation, though I could increasingly tell that something wasn't right. Taylor was reluctant to say anything for fear of how it would get back to his dad and stepmom, and I didn't want to lose the trust and connection we had.

When I picked him up from Plymouth, I looked for a deliberate ritual we could start so that we could have time together to talk about anything on our minds. We choose the Starbucks on the way back to his dad's house. It became one of our go-to places. Although I had limited parenting time through visitations, we did have Wednesday night car-talk and Starbucks time.

It was my understanding I had to invest in the long and stressful Child and Family Investigation legal process to be considered for 50/50 custody. Mike and I had to be observed and recorded by court-appointed professionals. It was horrible feeling, like I needed to prove that I was good enough to be a mom. The process was exhausting and nerve-wracking. The added expense of constant legal wrangling was traumatic to me, though I kept telling myself it wasn't a problem.

One part of the process involved hiring a Child Family Investigator (CFI). Deb Govan was the CFI assigned to us. She was direct, professional, and not easily swayed. She gathered information, scheduled personal observations, conducted in-depth interviews, and read letters requested from family and friends. Immediately upon completion, she recommended 50/50 custody. She also recommended their dad and I proceed with a court-appointed decision maker appointments to learn how to co-parent more effectively. I was thrilled to make progress in re-designing our family relationships. The impact, however, was not what I hoped for. Jonathan and Pamela were angry at the results, and the boys could feel the fury and resentment. At our best, the four of us were a D− as co-parents.

About once a month, I would still wake up between midnight and 3AM gasping for air. Some nights I couldn't even walk to the red Ford F-150 truck in our gravel driveway. Mike would carry my naked body to the truck, and then drape something across me as we raced to the ER. As he wheeled me into the hospital, my body would start an intensely predictable and violent routine. My normal breathing would escalate into a loud wheezing sound. I would gasp to get air in my lungs and exhale a tiny breath. As it became more and more difficult to breathe, I would then have an urgent need to have a forceful bowel movement—a violent expulsion of stool—then my breathing would very slowly restore itself. While in the ER, I would desperately whisper, "I need a pan to poop in" as the nurses walked around bewildered. They would offer an injection of something, and if the silver bed pan got there in time, the violent bowel movement would be self-contained. Otherwise, I made a mess and would collapse into a feeling of complete unworthiness.

As the boys were struggling to find their way back into their new life, I was trying to find my way, too. One early evening, I sat on the floor of the closet in our new home with my back sagging against the wall. The closet was dark, and my head drooped. I sat there feeling grateful for some things and still struggling with sadness and grief about something else, though I couldn't name it. I was out of options to resolve this breathing problem. I had been to allergy doctors and my regular physician. I told them my stress was minimal, though my airway was not big enough to swallow the air I needed at nighttime. I was referred to a specialist at National Jewish Hospital, where they asked if I might be experiencing anxiety. I said not a chance—I did yoga every week and had even started to understand the benefits of Shavasana. This is the pose I used to walk out on when I first started yoga, because it felt like a waste of time. With serious and intense practice, I could now lie flat on my back, find a place of physical comfort, close my eyes, focus on tranquility and remain there for 2 to 10 minutes, depending upon the instructor. I had all the evidence needed to prove to any health professional that anxiety was not remotely related to my inability to breathe late at night.

So, I didn't have a plan to solve my breathing problems.

In fact, I wore myself out trying to make a plan. There on the floor of our closet, I did the only thing left I could think of. I decided to hire a coach who was also a scientist. I had not had a coach since my training in 1999. I decided that I needed to find out how effective coaching could be when other lifelines were failing. In my own feeling of desperation, I screamed another silent prayer. I yelled: "Fine—Introduce me to a masterful coach who is an expert in neurology or another science, and I will pay the rate and connect in whatever time zone she lives and whatever language she speaks."

I did a Google search sitting right there on the floor, and the name Dr. Joan King popped up. I wrote down the message I wanted to leave on her recorder—in part so I didn't chicken out, chit chat about the weather, and avoid talking about what I wanted to talk about. I dialed the number, she picked up on the second ring, and I forgot what I was going to say.

She introduced herself and probably picked up on my reluctance to get too real too soon. She shared her background in years of spiritual studies in the Dominican convent where she was an instructor in chemistry and mathematics. She left the convent and entered graduate school to study science more deeply as a way to examine the substance of life and human behavior in what later became known as cellular wisdom. She became a professor at Tufts University Schools of Medicine in Boston for 20 years serving as Chair of the Department of Anatomy and Cellular Biology for the Schools of Medicine. Joan engaged in the scientific studies for nearly half a century before moving to Colorado and working internationally as a master coach.

"Where do you live in Colorado?" I asked.

She told me her address. She lived 12 miles away from my closet as the crow flies.

I told her I was sitting in my closet and couldn't figure out why my airway would shut down sometimes in the middle of the night. She told me the real story of why she left the convent. She had similar experiences of not listening to her body, and right there in that first conversation, she told me more about how she was able to utilize scientific principles as metaphors and tools in her own life and career as a master coach. "Life emerges from the energy that emanates from an individual's core beliefs and the focus of their thinking." I registered on the spot for her to be my mentor coach. I worked with Joan for six years, first as my coach and then she trained me to mentor coach others. In the first year, when she was my coach, she walked me through a short exercise to put my life purpose on paper. It went something like this:

"To create conversations that erase boundaries &

Cultivate a relationship with the unknown.

To invite each other to live more authentically, work more wholeheartedly &

Experience life naked without masks and to

Make a difference in the world by unleashing the power of love...."

Joan understood the brain and its functions. She could speak of neural mechanisms and the inner domains of people's experiences in a way that I personally felt seen and known. Joan impacted my life in profound ways before passing away from brain cancer in her home just over the ridge of red rocks in my own backyard. She had been there for years, though it took me collapsing in my own closet and inability to manage my breathing problems to reach out and discover this incredible Coach/Guide/Sage in our own backyard. Joan helped me to process things quickly, move forward, and integrate my life by taking control of my dreams.

During this same time, I discovered a therapist, Marilyn. Marilyn used EMDR (Eye Movement Desensitization and Reprocessing) in a collaborative approach with patients. At my first appointment with her, I got right to the point: "I do not think therapy is useful, though I have exhausted any medical resources I can think of. I don't want to be an ongoing inconvenience to Mike in the middle of the night, I don't want to be tired at work once a month, and I don't like the feeling these stupid things can happen when I'm traveling in other cities. I have asked an allergist, my primary physician, specialists in Denver, and a local bio-feedback specialist for something to make these breathing problems go away, and nothing has worked. Nothing! I have no other options, so I am here."

She took all of this in and then asked, "How will you know if EMDR works for you?"

"Well, that is easy. I will sleep through the night for one year without waking up unable to breathe or making a mess in the ER."

We met for a series of sessions, and nothing seemed to be changing. The appointments lacked any intensity, and I didn't cry. I kept waiting for some type of earth-shattering breakthrough. One day she asked me how my breathing was going. "Well, now that you mention it, I seem to have fewer breathing problems at night. Does that mean I'm making progress?"

"Yes, you are making tremendous progress. Our bodies keep score, and you are doing great at processing some of the hurts that you've pushed aside over the years."

Marilyn was a gentle soul. She created a safe environment for me to find my own way back into my own life. She granted me incredible permission. It took me multiple sessions to eventually tell myself I was a good mom and lay the tracks for living an even more authentic life personally and professionally.

Zachary was 17 years old, and all of his peers were making plans for graduation. He had been fully included in his high school experience and attended classes in chemistry, history, theatre, lunch, etc. Zachary established ordinary relationships with ordinary students, which supported his personal development. The literature and public policies show this approach to education also results in high school students being able to develop new kinds of social, civil, and educational skills they can use outside of the classroom.

After navigating many years of exploring ways for teachers, students, and parents to co-create inclusive classrooms, I was ready to celebrate Zachary's graduation from high school. Truth be told, since Zachary's birth, I had rehearsed this chapter of his life so much, I knew exactly what to do.

1. Order cap and gown.

2. Order cake with school mascot—the Saber Cats.

3. Look for decorations in his school colors: hunter green, silver, and black.

4. Tell family and friends date/time of graduation ceremony and his party.

5. Get ready to celebrate another major milestone: Yay!

His cap and gown came in, and I sneaked into the dress rehearsal for their graduation on campus at Colorado State University. The Moby Arena was fully renovated, including all-new seating and more than 23,000 square feet of hardwood flooring. The arena seated 8,745 people and was home to the wining CSU basketball team.

Walking into the arena, I could feel a surge of emotions inside of me. Since I had been thinking about this event since his first birthday, I was also prepared for a range of emotions. So, I focused on being in the moment and soaking up the energy as people whizzed by each other yelling instructions back and forth. I was awestruck by the timing of the whole event and the precision of organizing 639 kids to understand the rules of the big day and get everyone in sync.

I watched the teachers' aides guide the students from the back of the auditorium to the center aisle. I listened to the teachers connecting and congratulating students. I noticed a ring of seniors huddled around Zachary, and even I could feel the strange way they had walked in each other's shoes during their three years together. I noticed the mood of how graduation meant so many different things to so many different people. I could see the whole picture of how this special event was a series of beginnings, endings, anticipation, raging hormones, variations of maturity, and raw excitement.

I appreciated the staff who allowed me to vicariously witness the orchestration of this special event. I did my best to hide my tears, though each time the band started a song or a person greeted me by name, I cried harder. This was a rare moment where I was actually removed from the whole world of disabilities. I was in a public setting and watching Zachary live his life as a young man. I caught myself smiling. I felt an unexpected sense of freedom, as if all the limitations of his initial diagnosis had disappeared. Zachary belonged. For this brief moment, he belonged to a ritual, and he was immersed in his own experience.

The next day he finished his last day of high school with his peers, and I shopped at the Safeway grocery store to get food for his party.

The night before graduation, I felt still, quiet and full of thanksgiving. I felt thankful that Zachary was alive. I felt grateful for all the physicians, teachers, and care providers who were paid to be in his life and supported him to build friendships and a sense of belonging. I felt grateful for the people who were not paid to be in his life and loved him for who he was. I felt relieved that we had found our way through his high school years and had laid track for the next chapter of his life.

During that night, Zachary had 15 seizures, each one more intense than the last. His face was contorted. His eyes rolled back and he screamed louder and louder. Some parts of his body stiffened while other parts of his body twisted and jerked up and down and left and right. I sometimes worried that I needed to suction him so that he did not gag on his own saliva. In between his seizures, I sat beside him, and Mike sat beside me. We didn't speak. There was nothing to say.

Eventually we needed to decide if we should give him Diastat to interrupt the seizures or wait to see if they would stop on their own. They didn't stop; they increased in frequency and duration. We knew that in giving him the prescribed dosage, Zachary would sleep or be highly drugged for the next 24 hours and miss graduation.

Mike got the drugs. Zachary's seizures slowed down and then stopped.

We missed graduation, and I lost track of the outside world. Our dear family friends called from CSU's Moby Arena full of excitement and said, "Where are you?" I grabbed some words and felt terrible that I had forgotten to let them know we would not be there.

One of the things I learned over the years in raising Zachary was what happens when we enter the place of stillness. Stillness is one of the most powerful things in the universe. During the morning I felt anger. I felt sorry for Zachary and myself. I couldn't find any silver lining, and I didn't want anyone to find one for me. Grief washed over me.

Stillness, like breathing, was and is a source of life. Zachary was at peace and by the time we sat down to the breakfast table. I found my own moments of peace.

In fact, I had forgotten that we had invited our friends Paschal Karl and his wife Deb to spend the night with us. They were driving down from South Dakota and had scheduled an overnight stop in Fort Collins as part of a traveling equine photo service they owned. Paschal and Jan visited different parts of the west to take intimate photos of studs, weanlings, yearlings, and their owners in open spaces, arenas, pens, barns, or in the saddle on the trail. They had an innate talent for capturing the tender emotion of non-verbal communication.

I felt terrible for not calling our friends who went out of their way to come celebrate Zachary. I also felt a sense of unexpected grace when Paschal offered to take photos of Zachary later in the morning. Paschal captured Zachary's stillness and pure bliss in a series of photos outside on our front porch. To this day, they are the best graduation pictures I have ever, ever seen.

CHAPTER 13

CHANGES FOR ZACHARY
AND TAYLOR

As Taylor turned 16 years old, he moved from Boltz Junior High School to Fossil Ridge High School, the school in his dad's neighborhood and the school Zachary attended. It was 15.1 miles from our home in Bellvue, with largely upper-middle class Caucasian students and strong administrative leadership. The school had a contemporary vibe, and the student parking lot had Mazdas, Priuses, Volvos. Audis, and a few BMWs.

On the second day of school, Jonathan and I attended our bi-weekly mediation appointment. It was a typical session alternating between Jonathan being socially withdrawn and me desperately wanting to get to the heart of the issues blocking our teenagers' well-being.

The conversation began in a sterile and generic way, but within a short time, a terrible scene exploded. I was trying my hardest to approach the subject of Zachary and Taylor's rocky life gently. I could tell something was not right, and we just kept circling around the topic. I had made an agreement with Taylor that I would not disclose his experience or his observation of what was going on, though I did diplomatically acknowledge at this session that Taylor had run away from his dad's home. Jonathan had woken up in the middle of the night and gone downstairs to find Taylor was not there. He got in his car and found Taylor with a friend somewhere between running away, hitchhiking, and wondering if they should just go home while standing near Interstate-25 southbound.

Jonathan sat there steaming. I felt terrible for the awkwardness in front of the mediator, though I felt worse that the boys were feeling discounted in both subtle and blatant ways. I worried that I was breaking my agreement with Taylor, though I knew more that I needed to speak.

"You are the problem," Jonathan said. "You are the reason this isn't working."

"Jonathan, I am worried about the boys' well-being. They share a pink bedroom in the basement, are not involved in school activities, and Taylor could have been kidnapped out there in the middle of the night."

"You are a fuckin' bitch." He stood up and walked across the room. I couldn't remember ever hearing Jonathan curse like that. "You can have 100% custody of both boys, and I never want to see you again. Never come near me or my family ever again."

He picked up his briefcase, stared at me coldly for a moment, and then stormed out of the office. I felt terrible but also relieved that a little slice of truth had finally been spoken.

"What just happened?" I asked.

Kathleen, our court-appointed decision-maker, was a tall, slender woman with dainty rimmed glasses resting on her nose. She pushed her glasses up closer to her eyes and remained even-tempered and confident in her abilities. She watched Jonathan march out of the room. I looked the opposite direction out the window above the couch and tried not to shake.

"Jonathan may be doing the best he can. His anger may be the result of feeling like he has been wronged by people, or he may feel unable to assert his own needs. How are you feeling right now?" I trusted Kathleen and believed she had the boys' best interest as her focus. I did not feel a strong personal connection with her, though the courts considered her to be successful in helping families with difficult custody issues.

I sat still, trying to absorb what had just happened. Mike and I had never talked about full custody of both boys. All the research we had ever read stated that children needed strong relationships with their birth mom and dad.

"I'm feeling really scared. I'm scared that Jonathan thinks I've been trying to manipulate the situation to get the boys, and I am not. I'm scared the boys will think I am trying to take them away from their dad, and I am not. I'm scared about the well-being of the boys, and I don't know the solution."

Kathleen told me I was capable of doing this. It was near the end of our one-hour session, so she was direct. "Effective 5PM today, you will have 100% custody of Zachary and Taylor. I will notify the courts, and you will receive legal papers to sign and return."

"I know this a stupid question, but Mike and I were scheduled to fly to San Diego tonight to see his friend Gus and Nancy, who are 82 years old. What should we do?"

"You and Mike will need to figure that out. The important thing is to pick up Zachary and Taylor at 5PM tonight and spend time assuring them they are loved."

I got in my car and immediately called Mike. The conversation was short, and we moved into action. We agreed to 100% immediate custody of Taylor and requested maintaining 50% custody of Zachary until the age of 18 years old. Upon Zachary turning 18, I would become his legal guardian and assume 100% responsibility for him. Mike called Gus and Nancy to explain we needed to cancel our trip, and then we spent the weekend shooting pellet guns in the pasture and grilling burgers on the grill. We began to focus on our new norm as a family.

I needed to think quickly that weekend about which high school Taylor should attend. Given that he had just run away from his dad's home with a friend from nearby Fossil Ridge and I didn't know any of the families there, I made the decision for Taylor to start his high school experience instead at our neighborhood at Poudre High School. In fact, I had a strong suspicion that Taylor would have way too much unsupervised and idle time attending FRHS, and I needed to find a quick way to get Taylor connected into a local place of belonging. I had a strong gut feeling that it would make more sense for Taylor to be in proximity with the students, families, and neighbors of where we lived, rather than the more elite and upscale community where his dad had just moved. I knew from my own personal experience that feeling a sense of belonging trumped almost all other needs.

Poudre had 1,804 students and represented a lot of diversity, including a 22% Hispanic population and guys wearing cowboy hats and chewing tobacco. On Taylor's first day, I suggested he take the bus home. He had a transfer on the way, and as he waited at the transfer station, he watched another student get cornered and roped like a steer.

Our 1,200-square-foot modular home was small, with three bedrooms. Mike and I moved the desk and computer into our bedroom and set up one bedroom for Zachary and one for Taylor. Taylor and Mike became the "deconstruction-construction crew" and tore down the doorway into Zachary's room so we could easily get his wheelchair in and out. Zachary's room had posters of girls, bookshelves filled with science experiments from Barnes & Noble, and a digital fish tank. Taylor crammed his drum set in between his bed and desk. His closet door was made of mirrors, so it looked like he lived in a music studio.

Taylor was not happy about the initial move to PHS, though as time passed, the stress of a new school was replaced with the excitement of joining a Robotics team. The angst of not knowing anyone was replaced by connecting with two new friends. And the exhaustion of moving back and forth between two homes abated as he now called one place home. I felt horribly vulnerable and worked hard behind the scenes to support Taylor. I did not know families in the area, and I seemed to have forgotten how to reach out. In the moments when I had no idea what to do, I just did something…anything.

Ever since Zachary's early years, I had a timeline in my mind to raise him age appropriately. I had missed some opportunities while he lived in New Hampshire, but now I could get his life back on track. In my head there had been certain milestones for Zachary: For him to:

• Go to preschool and play	**Check!**
• Attend elementary school and get invited to a birthday party	**Check!**
• Participate in high school, go to prom and a football game, and graduate with a cap and gown	**Check!**
• Get dirty, take a risk, and break someone's heart	**Humm?**
• Get a car and get a job	**Working on adaptations**
• Move out at 18 years old	**Humm?**

Some of these milestones we had happily achieved, but I now had to figure out how the heck we could support Zachary to move out now that he was 18. I had a knack for starting conversations that were tied to big dreams like a kite. We were on track with my internal checklist, so the idea of him moving out of our home now that he was officially an adult seemed reasonable.

In March 2009, I met a man, Steve Espinoza. He was Zachary's case manager, and had compassion, empathy, and more kind-heartedness than I had ever met in a man employed by the human services division. He scheduled a meeting for Mike, Jonathan, and me.

On the day of the meeting, I suddenly didn't want to go. I hated when this happened, when my visions of possibilities and my feelings of inner chaos clashed. I felt like my choices were to either cancel the meeting or put a lot of effort into my own self-management so I didn't send a bunch of mixed messages. I opted to show up and manage my inner critic the best I could. When I arrived at the building, I signed in, got my nametag, and walked around until I found the meeting room. Jonathan and I had 50/50 custody of Zachary so it made sense that he would be there. As I walked in, I could sense the old feelings of stress permeate the room. Jonathan had made it very clear that did not want to be in the same room with me. So, the conversation had a rough start.

Then, out of nowhere, my vision of possibilities for Zachary collapsed. I sobbed and whispered to Steve about my feelings of shame and disgrace, and that I wanted Zachary to move into his own place with roommates like other guys his age. I asked Steve, how could I love Zachary so much, feel so invested in his life, yet want someone else to provide his daily care so that I could engage more fully with him in recreation, fun, and adventures like other young men? I wanted Zachary to track with other 18-year-olds, and I wanted to be fully engaged in supporting him to live that life. I had no role models for Zachary as young man with multiple disabilities or me as an aging mom.

Steve listened deeply. He listened beyond my words, and I could feel his empathy.

Jonathan was present throughout the entire conversation. He did not speak, though he was actively listening. I worked hard to create space for him to speak, though I think he was just relieved that I had established relationships with key stakeholders to try to navigate the next chapter of Zachary's life.

"If Zachary could live an ideal life, what it would be like?" Steve asked.

I appreciated the way Steve was helping me to try on other perspectives, though I had done extensive research, and outside of moving Zachary to Rhode Island, California, or Montana, I could not find any options in Colorado that were NOT depressing. The only local options I could find haunted me with images of residents with bed sores, drooling in their wheelchairs, watching frantic staff punching in and knowing they were overwhelmed, looking at cold food, and getting frustrated that people would baby-talk to Zachary like he was an infant.

So, the question about Zachary's ideal home setting stumped me. But then I let go of any angst I was feeling from others in the room. I let go of what didn't seem possible. I quieted all the noise in my head for a couple of short breaths and then said:

"The ideal place for Zachary to live would include three things: A home for him and a few roommates no more than 10 minutes away from our house. I need to know that I could see him, be with him, and jump in to assist with seizure management quickly. A home with a feeling of love, love, love. Zachary is highly empathic. He absorbs the emotions of people around him and in a healthy situation invokes compassion from others. He mirrors other people's positive vibrations and shuts down or disengages in places filled with fear and anxiety. He deserves to live in a home filled with love. And finally, he would need a home with a giant backyard—a colossal backyard with trees or water. If you can find a group home with these three things, that will be an ideal match for Zachary, though I must tell you this place does not exist."

Steve smiled kindly. He acknowledged how difficult this transition was and assured me that we would work together to find a solution for Zachary. I remember that day so well. I remember the long conference table and marks on the white board. I remember walking in with a split personality: One part of me had clarity on the next chapter of Zachary's life, and one part of me was enveloped with terror and anxiety. I remember how Steve met me where I was and guided the conversation so I left feeling whole.

Two weeks later, Steve called with an address. Mosaic Group Home was 10.1 miles from our home, backed up to the playground of Johnson elementary school, with walking distance to Westfield Park, Troutman Park, and Beattie Park. He asked if we would like to stop by and visit with the staff who worked there and the residents who lived there. I said I didn't know. I hung up and told Mike about it, and Mike asked if I wanted to go visit. I said I didn't know.

Mike recommended that we get in the car together later that week. He offered to drive and suggested we could just pass through the neighborhood. I agreed as long as I didn't need to get out of the car and wouldn't have to talk to anyone. I was still consumed with shame and doubt that I was a terrible mom for considering this idea. I worried if Zachary moved out of our home if he would feel abandoned. I was worried if he didn't move out, I would lose my mojo, and slowly we as a family would lose our mojo. I worried that we would tell ourselves a lie and silently wither away as our family aged.

We got in the car and drove by at about 15 mph. One of the residents was driving his power chair down the ramp. "Stop the car," I said. I looked at the man, and I looked at the ranch brick home. I noticed the three big trees in the front yard, and I could see the giant park in the backyard. I didn't say a word and just opened the car door. I got out and slowly walked toward the gentleman in the chair.

"Hello."

"Hello."

We walked in to visit, and the feeling of connectedness in the home surprised me. I did smell urine, and I did feel an element of heaviness in the air. I also felt a tiny ray of hope.

That August 2009 was Zachary's 18th birthday. We had made plans to celebrate him in the morning and then move him into his new group home. In my mental checklist, this had all the makings for an ideal day. The timing of Zachary moving out of our home was on schedule, as if he did not have a disability. The group home we chose for him was just right—it included the top three things that would support Zachary's well-being.

We showed up in the afternoon, and my heart sank. My original vision of what this next step would feel like disappeared. I felt ashamed and disappointed in myself. I did not have much experience of being with a concentrated number of people with disabilities. Over the past 18 years I had developed an awareness of "people first" language though I was always in places with a normal bell curve of diversity. I had developed a practice of viewing Zachary as my son who had many gifts, strengths, and characteristics, and one of his characteristics happened to be cerebral palsy. He was first and foremost "my son, Taylor's older brother," and never "my CP son."

Terra nullius is the Latin expression for "land belonging to no one"—and I felt like I was walking into a desert of emptiness, where no one belonged. I couldn't believe I had invested so much of my heart into seeing people first, yet here I was unable to see anyone. The house smelled like a nursing home, and most of the people living there appeared to be old, silent, and broken in some way. I hadn't even walked all the way into Zachary's designated room, yet I wanted to leave.

I glanced at Mike and said we should just drop off Zachary's things and then take him to Pappy's Corner Pub nearby to celebrate his birthday some more. Our family had lived in the apartments next to Pappy's a few years earlier while we were building our new accessible home. The waitresses all knew Zachary by name, what his favorite foods were, and they pureed his spicy bacon burger and fries. Pappy's felt more like home than this new foreign place.

We dropped off Zachary's belongings and then abruptly left, and I cried. I wept because this next step implicitly had everything my mind had focused on, yet something felt unnatural. Mike encouraged me to focus on the bigger picture. We talked about how this move would give us more capacity to do things in Zachary's life with him and support more systems of change for other people.

Zachary moved in and spent his first night. The staff was highly engaged, and his roommates were accepting of him. Mike attended the first two staff meetings. He introduced himself to the team while spinning Zachary in circles. Zachary squealed with delight, and Mike spoke about Zachary as a person. He described how he likes speed, girls, and spicy food. He said it was important to eliminate the space bubble and get physical, even the little things like fist bumping his shoulder when telling a joke. He talked about how to sit eye level, face Zachary with your heart to his heart, and make eye contact first and then chat about whatever you've got on your mind. Essentially Mike served as a bridge to encourage people to treat Zachary as an 18-year-old rather than a medically fragile man.

The staff picked up on ways to connect with Zachary. We worked with the leadership team to focus on important and natural community supports to maintain Zachary's physical, social, and mental well-being. We worked together to connect the dots so Zachary could use our family membership at the Raintree Health Club. The health club was only 2.6

miles from his new group home, and that was where he and I had been attending yoga classes since he was nine. Zachary started to attend the Yin Yoga class twice a week instead of the once a week. He swam at the Eldora Pool and Ice Center once a week to keep his heart rate healthy. Dennis scheduled training runs and worked with me and the team to transport Zachary to upcoming races.

Each time I went to visit Zachary, I set aside time to meet and connect with each of his new roommates. They were much older, many in their 50s or 60s. I tried to sit eye level and face each person heart to heart, though sometimes I just wanted to scoop up Zachary and get outdoors. I told myself that ever since I was a single mom, I had this urgency to make sure Zachary got outside for a walk every day. Every day no matter what—and walking to the end of the driveway and back counted. Since the staff wasn't able to do this each day, I rationalized this was my focus. Sometimes that was an excuse. Sometimes it was difficult for me to see Zachary living in a place that was not a "natural" setting. Usually I struggled to straddle the three different worlds of living in an unnatural setting like a group home, living in my own world as it existed, and the world I knew it could be. I met so many compassionate people of all abilities along the way, though being present in the spaces where people were marginalized saddened my heart.

The house managers did a lot to manage the complexities of reducing turnover and keeping everyone up to date on protocols, procedures, rules, and regulations. The team worked hard to provide safety, medical care, and daily care, and in between create moments of connection. Together we co-created a lot of good memories, and there were even times they saved Zachary's life. On more than one occasion, someone observed a small change in Zachary's behavior and called the residential nurse, who advised he get in to see the doctor. Often this led to getting admitted to the hospital for a series of unexpected outcomes. Zachary would live there for more than five years, and I just kept showing up one day at a time to say hello and celebrate anything that was going right.

Meanwhile, Taylor was making strides to adjust to high school life. Mike and I decided it was important for Taylor to get a job so he could begin to experience independence. Taylor applied and was offered two jobs. He served meals at an Assisted Living home for the elderly a few afternoons a week and mopped floors—including the blood in the butchery unit and grease from the chicken fryers—at the local grocery store after closing. Taylor showed signs of accepting challenges, establishing new relationships, and exploring a sense of meaningfulness in his life. He did not go to visit Zachary at the group home much, though he didn't miss a family dinner or activity when the four of us scheduled time together. It felt natural and good to be together as a family of four.

Taylor tried to maintain a connection with his other family also in Fort Collins, though he was often treated like an imposter. One day he came over to visit as planned and could not get into the house, even the garage code had been changed. So, rather than riding a bicycle home, he sat on the front step and just waited. The feeling of being a threat to others, unworthy and unloved in their home continued.

By the time Taylor moved in with us full-time and started high school, he had moved 11 times and had also lived between two homes seven of those years. Like me, Taylor would go to great lengths to accommodate people's expectations and step around conflict which induced additional stress and anxiety.

In the summer of 2007, Taylor agreed to attend MADD summer camp at La Foret in Colorado Springs. When we initially pulled into the registration parking lot and he saw the poster "Music Art Drama & Dance" he decided he was not getting out of the car. I had not exactly mentioned the theory of MADD was to support teenagers to get in touch with God through the arts. MADD had a focus of getting teens "out of their heads" and into experiencing the transcendent. He did eventually get out of the car, probably because we both wanted to avoid any conflict with each other. During that first summer, I heard Taylor talking about the kinds of moments that worked for him to more authentically develop his life-long spiritual path. As much as I hated pushing him out of the car on the first day, I loved picking him up on the last day. I loved listening to his completely unfiltered monologue of girls, God, running in a rainstorm at midnight, girls, counselors initiating topics avoided in mainstream life, girls, and the Thursday night dance.

As high school graduation approached, I started to think about ways to support Taylor in the next chapter of his life. His great grandmother, my grandmother, had graciously given him her 1996 Mercury Sable car for his 16th birthday. We had given him a new computer at Christmas in preparation for college. I thought about my own experience of people and things that had helped to center me in times of big changes. I thought about people who had characteristics of being grounded and attuned to their own internal compass. I wondered how I could bundle something like that into a box with a bow.

So, I did what came naturally to me. I started to listen for ideas about a graduation gift for Taylor from all different sources. It happened as I was sitting in line at a Starbucks drive-thru. I was talking on my cell phone with Cheryl, Taylor's former preschool teacher. She also happened to be an instructor for Transcendental Meditation, and we had stayed in touch over the years. She was encouraging me to register for the upcoming TM meditation training. She reminded me of the benefits of daily meditation. Cheryl gave me the website of a Stanford University meta-analysis of 146 independent studies proving that meditation was an effective method to reduce stress and anxiety. By the time I was ready to place my coffee order at the window, I finally heard her. After many years of gently suggesting I learn TM, I finally asked if I could go ahead and register Taylor and me to attend the meditation training.

Over the years, Taylor and I had developed a series of approaches to stay connected. We stumbled into conversations we never saw coming, walked the dogs through Lory State Park, and took annual road trips to Spirit Lake by driving through the night. Each of those was a moment we could co-create together. The idea of learning meditation together seemed to me, however, to be an invitation for each of us to grow our own deeper practice of physically, spiritually, and mentally letting go of some things and getting centered in other things.

On the day of Taylor's high school graduation, I gave him a mother/son gift certificate to learn TM. Although the gift may have been a little anti-climactic for him, we chose a date and attended the training.

Students nationwide with disabilities are fully supported to attend high school until the age of 21. The students and staff at Fossil Ridge High School were phenomenal, so Zachary kept attending his high school for an extra three years even after he graduated. When Zachary turned 21 years old, he would need to leave Fossil Ridge High School. At 21, typically people with multiple severe disabilities were assigned to a local agency to be taken care of during the day in "day programs." People in "day programs" often gathered in groups of 7–15 people and went to Wal-Mart or some other place and called it "community involvement." (Note: Mosaic, the agency that supported Zachary's group home, locked the doors during the daytime. They did not provide services to residents during the daytime.)

This idea felt grave to me. There had to be ways to leverage the same budget to explore other options for Zachary and others to live meaningful lives as adults with disabilities. I felt an urge to find someone else who would be willing to create other possibilities.

Zachary's case manager was now Kim, Steve's wife. Kim provided oversight for adults with disabilities after they turned 21. As with many high school students, this is a critical point in the lives of young adults. Some go to college, some attend vocational programs, some work in a family business, and others stumble through those next years from one job to the next. Some students follow their friends and live paycheck to paycheck; some explore work that might lead to meaning and purpose. For young adults with disabilities, many either attend a sheltered workshop or get matched with a job coach. Sheltered workshops had a reputation for being exploitative, abusive, and discriminatory. Research showed that "hundreds of thousands of people with disabilities were being isolated and financially exploited by entities authorized to employ workers with disabilities at sub-minimum wages.[6]" By 2011, the Attorney General of the Civil Rights Division of the US Department of Justice would publicly take a position that people with disabilities needed to be supported to live meaningful lives, not spend their lives in congregate programs isolated from the world. I remember attending a meeting in the building that hosted the largest sheltered workshop-type setting in Northern Colorado, and vowed that Zachary would never have to participate, though he was not prepared to enter the typical job market, either. There was a big gap and limited options.

---

[6] www.michigan.gov/.../mdch/Segregated-and-Exploited

I asked Kim if she had any suggestions. She said there were a few agencies in town who provided "day programs."

"What the heck is a day program?" I had never attended one of these. Neither had Mike or Taylor, so I didn't even know what we were talking about.

"It's a program organized by an agency selected to spend government dollars to support a person with a disability between 9AM and 3PM."

I asked her if she would tell me which agencies were still working in the Stone Age and just collecting a paycheck and which agencies were invested in doing the right thing.

"Well," Kim asked. "What is your definition of doing the right thing?"

"We are looking for an agency that develops staff who practice things themselves and then practice the same things with the customers who purchase their services. I'm thinking of core things like: Positive attitude, engaging in meaningful lives, developing real relationships, and getting creative about how to give back each day."

She gave us a list of 16 agencies each promoting their services to support adult people with disabilities 9AM–3PM weekdays. Each of them accepted public funding and worked locally. I called each of them and asked a few simple questions:

1. What is your vision for people with severe disabilities?

2. How can we as a family support your vision and mission?

3. How successful are you in your vision, and what is your evidence?

Some agencies called back that week. One didn't call back at all. But one executive director called back the same day and asked if we were interested in getting together to chat. His name was Jessie Otero, who owned the Otero Corporation. The Otero Corp. was one of the 16 agencies accepting public funds to support people with intellectual or physical disabilities and providing things like "residential services" and "day habilitation".

Over beers at Pappy's, Jessie asked us powerful questions and then kicked back and listened with his entire being. He asked us things like:

1. What are your dreams for Zachary?

2. What else is important to us as an agency to think about regarding Zachary's future?

3. What would an ideal day be for Zachary? He asked us to be specific.

Then, are you ready for this? He said that their agency had only supported clients with intellectual disabilities, never one with physical disabilities, so this opportunity could induce some pressures on the team and they were ready for it. They did not have any vehicles with wheelchair lifts, though they did have leaders and staff who worked collaboratively and passionately to create a world of possibilities.

Jessie had a lot of experience in the realm of adult services and witnessed patterns from what leadership guru Ronald Heifetz calls the "balcony." I was attracted to leaders who could succinctly move between the big picture of a situation and the details to get things done. Jessie was able to metaphorically climb up into the balcony of Zachary's life and look down onto the situation through the lens of this broader perspective. Rather than being caught in the small details of what could and could not be done, Jessie, unlike other agency directors, was able to talk about a vision for Zachary (the balcony) and the day-to-day actions any agency could take to support him in living that vision. Heifetz refers to this as moving back and forth between the balcony and the dance floor. He describes how critical it is to have the capacity to move between the day-to-day action and the ability to rise above that and reflect and focus on the bigger picture.

Jessie had the leadership and operational experience of running a non-profit organization that we as a family did not have. As a family, we had an attunement to Zachary's hopes, dreams, and well-being. Jessie and I felt an immediate connection and put together a plan for Zachary to join the Otero team during the day. Jessie got his team together to talk about the amazing challenge of bring someone with a physical and cognitive disability into their program. I worked with the Mosaic staff to talk about transportation and communication in working with a team other than the sheltered workshop place other residents attended during the day. Together, the Otero team, the Mosaic team, Dennis from Athletes in Tandem, Zachary's yoga instructor, and others designed a relationship focused on listening and learning from each other. Zachary began spending his weekdays with the Otero team. New partnerships took flight, new adventures got started, and amazing things happened in extremely ordinary ways.

CHAPTER 14

NEVER A DULL MOMENT

Colorado in May is never dull. We have had snowstorms on Mother's Day, and it has also been 90 degrees. Sometimes I like the surprises of living here. Sometimes I yearn for more predictable and ordinary moments.

Taylor finished his freshman year at University of Colorado in Boulder in May 2012. He had A's and B's his first semester, so it never occurred to me to ask about his second semester. Taylor and I had an agreement that I would pay all of his room/board/tuition/fees for four years. For his part, Taylor would study an area he chose and would maintain A's, B's or C's, though if his grades were lower, he would pay the next semester tuition. So, after being home for a couple nights at the beginning of summer break, he briefly asked if he could go camping with guys from high school before starting his summer job and added, "Oh, by the way. I just looked online, and it appears I failed a couple of classes." I was shocked. I said no to camping with his friends and then was at a loss for words.

Taylor negotiated to go camping one night. I agreed so that Mike and I could pow-wow about consequences of his poor performance. When Taylor came home, I was at the kitchen table, fuming. My heart rate was increased, my muscles tense, and I felt equal parts hurt and scared. I didn't have spare money for an extra semester of classes. All I could say was, "You need to register for summer school, live at home, and work full time." I said it with a dramatic overtone of "Good luck with that." Then I turned around and walked away.

I said I would pay his tuition for summer semester because all the gremlins in my head said, "Oh, my God—he is going to end up homeless on the streets without an education." When I gave birth to these kids, I told myself they would have full access to education and outdoor recreation no matter what it took, so I told myself, "He is going back to school to study something he wants. NOW."

Mike had his own way of handling Taylor. One of the recommendations of the counselor I had seen was to butt out of Mike and Taylor's relationship. I told her I would, though I didn't. I used fewer words, though I still tried to facilitate animated family conversations at the dinner table. Mike, Zachary, and Taylor played along.

Mike worked to please me while also finding his own path to strengthen his relationship with Taylor. When Taylor was 14, Mike had asked him to drive the Ford F-150 truck in the pasture. He had built a man cave above the barn with a refrigerator as a place for Taylor and his friends to hang out. Mike had been deliberate in setting aside time for him and Taylor to talk as men and has never revealed what they talked about. Mike was highly invested in Taylor. He was also on alert for signs of disrespect. He could smell pot, find a bottle, or tell me it wasn't OK after the police called on a Saturday night. In times of stress and pressure, Mike had a tendency to react and yell, and then I would interpret his mood as an indicator of our family falling apart. Forever.

That summer when Taylor was home, he said something under his breath. Mike gave me the look of anger and disappointment and left to go mend the fence. Taylor and I had a pattern of avoiding any further escalation of the moment and would usually just sit quietly. Eventually, one of us would say something to re-stabilize a fake, and positive, mood.

On this day, Taylor headed toward the door. "I'm going outside to talk with Mike."

"Taylor—don't. Just don't."

He put on his shoes and walked outside. I made the decision for the first time to listen to my counselor and not be a part of the bloodshed that was about to happen.

Instead I waited 10 minutes and silently slid open the back sliding glass doors. As I rounded the back of the house, I could hear Mike yelling and Taylor standing there listening. Then I saw Taylor put his arms in the air and yell back. They were 50 yards away, and I could hear their voices, though not their words. I stood there watching as long as I could. I then abruptly turned around and ran into the back door of the house. I went to the bathroom to take a shower. I could cry hardest in the shower. I could sob with my whole body and not hear myself. I stood and sobbed that my family had completely disintegrated into rubble.

As I stood in the shower exhausting myself, I heard a knock on the bathroom door. I ignored it.

"Mom, are you in there?"

Silence.

"Mom, it's me. Can we talk? I love you."

Eventually I turned the hot shower off. I slowly grabbed a towel to wipe my face. I put on a robe and cracked the door open and didn't say a word.

"Mom, Mike and I are good. We just had to say some things to each other that we've never said. We gave each other big hugs and then Mike told me to get up here and find you. Can you come out?"

I was stunned.

How could it be that a bloodbath could be healing among two men that I loved, though I had always felt an element of tension between them?

I had struggled so many times to understand when to take a stand and when to let go. I had worked so hard to learn the distinctions of how to protect my children from points of pain and when to step back as they navigated the next step in their path.

I was still in foreign territory, though I got dressed. Mike came up, and the three of us sat at the kitchen table. I didn't say a word. I listened to them tell me what happened and their request of me. They told me that they loved me, though I needed to give them space rather than protecting, triangulating, or whatever else I did. I needed to have more faith in each of our abilities to be open, honest, and transparent in our one-on-one relationships.

Mike told Taylor a little inside secret he and I had. It came from watching the movie *Avatar*. At the end of the movie, the main character says to the 10-foot tall blue-skinned humanoid, "I see you." Mike said that to me after the movie, and I smothered him with hugs saying, "I feel so connected when you say that." Mike responded by sticking out his index finger. I wasn't sure what to do, so I stuck out my index finger. He touched my index finger with his and said, "Now we're connected, and I see you." It felt so special at the time, though a bit corny describing it to Taylor. We rotated holding out our index fingers with each other in a moment to see each other.

Taylor left early each morning to work eight hours, drive 90 minutes to Boulder, attend class, drive 90 minutes back and do homework. Mike and I went to work, and I would stop by Zachary's house to visit him on the way home every few days and check in on the team. Zachary was increasingly showing signs of very subtle behaviors that didn't quite seem normal. He just wasn't being himself.

One morning the staff took him to see his doctor, and I met him at the clinic. The doctor did a physical exam, though nothing seemed out of the ordinary. The phlebotomist drew some blood, ran some tests, and when the results came back four hours later, Zachary was immediately admitted as an inpatient at the hospital.

By the next day, Zachary was lying in bed on the third floor of the hospital in the corner room. We had been in this room before. After a series of poking, prodding, doctors, nurses, specialists, and x-ray technicians rotating in and out of our room, the doctor said Zachary's condition was very serious and extremely complex. They were not sure of his diagnosis, though they were sure it was not good. The best guess until further notice was some type of full-body cancer. Zachary and I spent the night alone in the room, and I could not even wrap my head around what they were saying. I felt exactly like I had the day 21 years before on the same floor of the same hospital, when I took my healthy baby into the ER and walked out with a diagnosis of severe brain damage and likely death by age one. I felt too heavyhearted to call anyone except Mike, who came to the hospital to silently sit beside us.

The next morning, the doctors came in with good news and bad news. The good news was that he did not have cancer. That was all I heard. I smiled and just held Zachary as we collapsed into each other's bodies in that hospital bed. We both fit in the bed as long as I lay on my side. I could feel myself breathing, and I could feel Zachary breathing. Time stopped completely still, and we had breathing space.

By that afternoon, a cardiac surgeon came to Zachary's room, and we had a conference with the whole team of pediatricians, nurses from night shift and day shift, phlebotomists, pharmacist, certified nurse assistants, social workers, and others. The room was quiet as the staff walked into Zachary's room single file.

The pediatric cardiologist began: "Zachary has a blood clot attached to a stem in the lower left ventricle of his heart."

Silence. Mike looked at me and asked if he could ask a question aloud that might be difficult for me to hear. "Of course," I whispered.

"What size is the blood clot?" Mike was observing the large number of people in the room and deducted that this was a big deal. The cardiologist answered the question then added, "I've been in practice over two decades and never seen one this size before."

"It sounds like a large mass," Mike said. The cardiologist team nodded. I trusted they knew what they were talking about, though any number smaller than one didn't sound too scary. All my life fractions or percentages less than one I just rounded down to zero.

The decision was to have a team from the hospital transport him by ambulance to the Children's Hospital in Denver where Zachary had been admitted before. They talked about which IVs needed to stay in his veins and which medications needed to be transported with him. I agreed to follow the ambulance to Denver. Admitting a 21-year-old to a children's hospital is a rapidly growing challenge in the world of medicine. It was becoming a relatively new issue because children with multiple complex medical issues were beginning to live longer than original diagnosis of 1–5–10 years. We had not discussed any transition plan to transfer Zachary's thick medical records or develop a relationship with a new team of adult physicians. Furthermore, the literature showed that many physicians do not feel competent caring for young adults with complex medical needs, in part because they see patients like this so infrequently and do not have a personal history or emotional connection. Our pediatrician had initiated this topic, though I had ignored or discounted the idea of transferring to a strange new practice.

Mike stayed in Bellvue to take care of the animals and eat dinner with Taylor each night when he got home from his 150-mile/15-hour days.

Taylor had no social life and was denying that his college social life last semester was the cause of his exhausting summer routine.

Zachary's diagnosis was considered rare and a "reportable." When I asked what reportable meant, the physician kindly explained it was extremely rare to find a blood mass attached to the left ventricle wall. It needed to be reported to the state, where they collect statistics on unusual and rare diagnoses. Later we would be asked permission for Zachary's case to be presented at a regional conference. We were told that one of the dangers was that if this massive blood clot had any infarctions or pieces break off and float upstream, he would have a stroke and die.

As the doctor spoke, I heard "Blah, blah, blah…. Any questions?" In times of stress, I can appear like I am listening, though I actually can't hear anything. Unlike 21 years ago, when Zachary was first diagnosed and I put all of my effort to acting like I was listening and wanting people to think I was a good mom, I now had the courage to smile and say, "Can we sit down? Would you talk to me some more? Could you tell me what words to write down so I can understand this later? I know I look like I am listening, but I'm not really hearing you."

Surgery was scheduled to happen in two days. I called Jonathan to tell him the unexpected news. "Jonathan, Zachary has a serious heart condition, and we are at Children's Hospital in Denver. This is not about you and me. This is about Zachary's life and Zachary's well-being."

"I heard you."

"Jonathan, I've been advised there is a possibility that Zachary may not survive this surgery. He will need to go on a ventilator and his heart will be stopped in a cold room during the surgery. It is a possibility that he could die."

Silence. Then, in a quiet voice, Jonathan said, "I asked you not to call me."

Click. That was the end of the conversation.

My sister Kristin drove down to spend the day with Zachary before surgery. I drove back to Ft. Collins to pack things in preparation for spending a few nights in the Denver hospital. It would also give me a chance to eat dinner with Mike and Taylor and give them an update on Zachary.

The three of us sat on the back porch up against the steep red rock cliff that bordered our back yard. Mike was opening the mail and trying to figure out why he got a speeding ticket he had no memory of. The ticket showed a photo of his car and a close-up of his license plate. He took off his glasses and held the ticket inches away from his face to get a closer look.

"This isn't me. This is YOU driving my car through a red light!"

I hated the teachable moments when I was in the wrong, and both Taylor and Mike got to watch me squirm. As we sat around our porch table, Mike and Taylor decided that whenever someone in the family did something wrong, the rest of the family got to assign that person a nickname.

"Let's call her James Bond."

"No way—that's not a feminine name."

"Okay—let's call her Jasmine. Jasmine Bond."

I said no, though I had no voting rights.

The evening was lighthearted. I had made my first batch of baked kale chips in the oven and carried them out the back sliding-glass doors. As I stepped outside, a light breeze scattered them in the air and around the porch like ashes from a fire. I snatched a couple of the edible ashes for Mike and Taylor to eat. They were relieved the rest had blown away. We noticed a giant cloud of gray smoke way off in the distance to the northwest of us. Eventually, it got dark and we went to bed. I was emotionally exhausted, though happy to be home for the night.

At 4:45AM, the sky was an eerie dark fog. We jumped out of bed to the screech of sirens. I ran out the sliding glass doors of the front porch to the feeling of a spooky haunted house. The typical morning sunlight was replaced with a ghostly and frightening scene. The police were driving up our ¼-mile gravel driveway with lights piercing the smog and a speaker telling us we needed to leave. The fire was just over the hill from us, and this was an emergency evacuation.

I can remember, just like in yoga, how to take a deep breath and begin a new pose which could open me up to new perspectives. I did my best yoga breath, assumed the perspective that everything was going to be all right, looked around, and knew immediately what I needed to do. I:

1. Stuffed my gym bag with toiletries and undies.

2. Filled Zachary's tub with water. I figured this was one of the most important features of our home to Zachary and I could save it by filling it with water.

3. Grabbed a mini suitcase and packed it with all the photo CDs I'd made at Walgreen's.

4. Grabbed the cellphones and computers and their power cords.

I put the stuff in the back seat of my Subaru. The back hatch area of my car was empty, though I couldn't think of anything else we needed. I asked Taylor if he needed help. He packed his computer and notebooks for summer classes and put them in his car. Mike was busy protecting the house by strategically putting large garbage buckets of water along the perimeter. When we'd built our new wheelchair accessible home a few years before, Mike had insisted on a metal roof, stucco exterior, and we maintained a small dirt pasture near the home for fire protection. He loaded the safe with all of our legal documents into the Ford F-150 red truck. He gathered other documents from a locked file cabinet, and we left everything else behind.

I drove three hours in traffic to the Children's hospital and got there by 8:30AM. My sister was sitting with Zachary. She had brought essential oils like bergamot, clary sage, eucalyptus, and lavender to massage Zachary's quadriplegic, spastic, boy-man body. She was a massage therapist and could convert a hospital room into a healing sanctuary, awaking all the senses. I plopped into the hospital chair and told her about our family being evacuated and the uncertainty of what would happen to our home.

Within 24 hours, Zachary was having a significant spike in his seizure activity, and the clusters were closer together during the day and night. On a typical day, Zachary would have 0–3 seizures while sleeping, though he was now having 25 in 24 hours, and the intensity was escalating. I asked the nurse if he was getting all of his seizure medications. She was confident and said yes. Taylor came by after class and asked if he was getting his seizure medications. I said something wasn't right and asked him to trust his gut and ask the staff anything he wanted to ask. Taylor approached a different nurse and was told Zachary was getting all of his seizure medications. She also seemed confident. I cried that night feeling helpless. I felt scared about what to take a stand on and what to let go of. The less sleep I had, the stronger my personal convictions were, though I was losing my filters and ability to discern what was happening. The next night, I begged the resident on call to reach out to the senior cardiac surgeon. He did not call him, though early the next morning, when the cardiac surgeon came in for 6:00AM rounds, I pleaded for him to listen to me. I felt heard by him. He did not know the source of this new problem, though he did recommend we postpone surgery until this new seizure problem was resolved.

In the end, there was a medication error—a human error. There was a mistake in transferring the list of seizure medications from the first hospital to the ambulance that brought him to the Denver hospital. No harm was done. My confidence in trusting myself was slowly restored.

Six days after being admitted, Zachary had the open-heart surgery, and the team provided excellent patient care. Zachary and I lived in the Cardiac Intensive Care Unit.

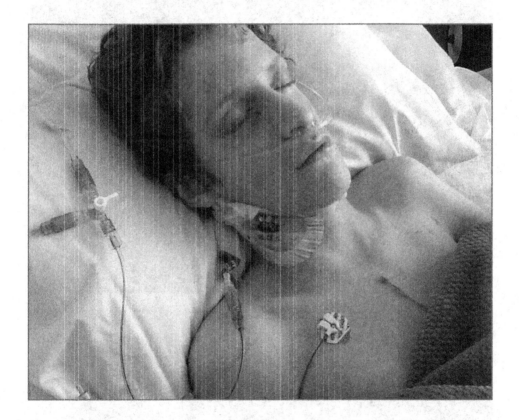

Meanwhile, the High Park fire raged up and down the mountain range where we lived in Bellvue, fueled by the blue spruce and white pine trees. The reports showed torched trees burning across the street from our home. The fire burned over 87,284 acres, destroyed at least 259 homes, and would become the second-largest fire in recorded Colorado history. (Black arrow pointing to our home).

Mike lived in a rotation of friends' homes and hotel rooms between midnight and 5:00AM, and attended fire meetings and took care of the animals from 5:00AM to midnight. Taylor drove a daily triangle between Boulder for summer school, Denver to visit Zachary, and Bellvue to eat dinner with Mike. They focused on staying updated on the fire damage at the different command centers.

Zachary and I sat together in a quiet place of bliss. In the absence of talking or TV or other distractions, something else filled the room. We felt a mutual sense of presence. Each time we silently made eye contact, our connection deepened. It was becoming increasingly natural to feel the awkwardness of nothing to do or focus on and then sink into a place of peace together. I wondered if I could ever find my way back to the on-ramp of such a busy and chaotic life. In a backwards way, any anxiety I had softened, and I felt anchored in a new place of mindfulness. I could feel the presence of what the spiritual master Thomas Merton meant when he suggested that deep communication is not communication at all, rather a sense of communion.

I made arrangements for Zachary to take a bath, and we talked about our upcoming "spa day." I told him he would be able to do one of his favorite things—float and soak in a giant tub of warm water. I washed his boy-man body slowly, with the sound of birds, flutes, and acoustic guitars on my portable speaker. We spent most days looking out the window together, rotating between the intimacy of silence or exploring new music on Pandora. During the course of three weeks, we watched one movie three times—*Soul Surfer* with Dennis Quaid, Helen Hunt, and Carrie Underwood. The rest of our days were filled with the simplicity of being.

Mike got notification that the fire had turned back on itself and was retreating away from our neighborhood. He and Taylor were able to show identification, pass the National Guard barricade to our neighborhood, and begin cleaning the soot and vacuuming the walls and floors. Late that same afternoon, Taylor went to visit my dad, his grandfather, for Father's Day. He left his books and computer in the house and said he would be back in a few hours. Within those few hours, the wind changed direction and the fire headed back for our neck of the woods. Taylor was not allowed past the barricade, and everyone was forced to evacuate again. When the police pounded on the front door of our home, Mike didn't answer. He locked himself in and did not show any signs of movement. During the daytime he peeked out the windows to keep track of what was happening. At night he used a small flashlight to take care of critical things. Mike had taken survival classes and horse camped with limited supplies. He was able to take care of his basic needs and protect our home in the event that the fire jumped the road.

Taylor stayed with Zachary and me at the hospital, and on occasional nights when my sister was able to spend the night, Taylor and I would get a hotel room in Boulder, close to his classes. He needed to pass the chemistry and engineering course, regardless of the evacuation and open-heart surgery.

I didn't know how long I was going to be missing work at Banner Health. Each time I started to stress about getting behind, my colleagues would tell me just to focus on my family. I believed them and will be forever grateful. It never occurred to me later how helpful it would have been for me to have someone like their dad take a shift so I could sleep in a bed somewhere. But Jonathan had said he never wanted to see me again, and apparently this situation was no exception.

The day Zachary was discharged from the hospital was the same day we could move back into our home. To this day, when I sit on our front porch, I see the burn line right across the street. The evacuation became a powerful metaphor to me. At first I wrestled with what it meant. Then it came to me like a bolt of lightning. I realized there were relationships across the spectrum of my life that needed to die so that rebirth could happen. I had an immediate awareness of a team I was leading that felt like a chain, and I needed to move on. I called the executive director of the entrepreneurial venture named *Executive Career Hub* and resigned from my role as a master coach. I initiated a tough conversation with two colleagues and another person employed by the disability industry. I wanted to move on and take my life back in a healing way.

I wondered how many times I thought it was my job to prop up all relationships and teams no matter how unhealthy they were. I no longer believed that. I started to believe that sometimes it would be better to let them go their own ways, perhaps even dissolve. It takes less effort to let go of things so that new ideas, new thoughts, new relationships can find their way into the world.

Within two weeks, I could hardly believe how much neon-colored fresh bright grass had started to peek up among the rich and scorched black soil.

I had admired thought leaders like Ronald Heifetz and others who taught some version of a "holding environment." Each one had a definition of how a holding environment supported better outcomes through the lens of leadership, business, and making the world a better place. Some people refer to a holding environment as a "psychological space that is both safe and uncomfortable." In the realm of coaching, it is a series of conversations that support a person or team to experiment with a new way of being.

In my coach training, I'd studied Robert Kegan's Levels of consciousness. He maintains that we need a "holding environment" to assist us as we mature into the next stage of human development. When someone creates a holding environment for us, they support our current stage of development and encourage our movement to the next evolution of who we are becoming. Kegan describes a holding environment similar to an "evolutionary bridge, a context for crossing over from one order of consciousness to the next, more developed order." Most of us as adults experience the first four stages of development, though fewer than 15% of adults engage in the journey of a fully integrated adult.

So, my desire to become one of America's Top 10 Physician Coaches became the closest thing I could name for the next step on my path. It came from my own personal experience of noticing how the people in the world of medicine had most impacted our family and me. As physicians touched our life and impacted Zachary's capacity to live beyond the initial diagnosis of probable death, I found myself wanting to give back almost as a form of devotion. I was curious how I could author my own life in such a way that I could co-create a holding environment for the physicians, patients, and parents to re-connect with their souls. I wondered how we might create holding environments for each other as people on the path to heal ourselves and each other.

I started to invest more time in noticing where I was putting my attention. I began coaching boldly from my own deeper knowing. I included poetry, wilderness, wordlessness, and music. I allowed new thought leaders in the realm of leadership, sociology, business, and economics to influence me more. I got out of my own way and took a stronger stand for the people in my life: friends, family, clients.

As I continued to provide individual, small, and group coaching experiences for physicians and executives, I started to hear people give voice to their own insights. I heard physicians reflect on their own insights about managing themselves in new ways and understanding leadership in new ways. I heard comments like:

- "I want to get a better understanding of my strengths and how to run with them."

- "It just occurred to me that I cannot understand others until I have a deeper understanding of myself."

- "I thought we were supposed to cover up our weaknesses; now it makes sense to learn more about them."

- "I really don't know myself outside my role of studying medicine."

- "I didn't realize I am responsible for my career path—sounds crazy, though I have been on auto-pilot."

The great teachers suggest that we cannot see something if we start with a "no" mindset. We must cultivate a sense of wonder and curiosity by beginning with "yes." We need to enter an open field. So, I wanted to find a way to connect with Taylor by practicing some of the coaching skills I had learned, while being sensitive to not "coach" him. Mike and Taylor both hated when I "coached" them, rather than simply hung out as me. I wanted to focus on the opportunity for me to practice meeting Taylor where he was and walk beside him in the conversation of his life. During Taylor's junior year in college, he and I sat on the porch in rocking chairs overlooking the Rocky Mountains. He confessed that he was dreading a career in a cubicle and stacks of papers. He had lost interest in the engineering careers other people talked about. We shifted the conversation to talk about what it might be like to be an engineer in a state of flow. We talked about leveraging his values, his strengths, and his personal aspirations.

By the end of the conversation, Taylor walked to the other side of the 25-yard porch. He flipped open his laptop, and his eyes lit up. Later that night I watched the twinkle in Taylor's eyes as he described his future. He wanted to earn an entrepreneurial certificate, travel internationally, and work through science and conversations to bring real-life solutions to real-life people. During the next 18 months, he blended entrepreneurship courses with his engineering classes and fully engaged in his own TM practice of daily meditation. He launched a start-up company with three colleagues and participated in a nine-week startup accelerator designed to help students with promising ideas and technologies succeed. They traveled to Nicaragua to do research with rural farmers and test their solar panels designed to bring affordable water to farmers living close to poverty.

As Taylor fully engaged in his new passion for education and a vocation, I along with a small team of folks noticed that Zachary was once again not quite being himself. He seemed increasingly sluggish and disengaged. One of Zachary's super-powers was to match or mirror the energy of other people, so I wondered if he was feeling lonely. I stopped by on a Saturday afternoon to spend more time with him and felt completely inadequate that we couldn't connect. He looked exhausted and absent of any physical or emotional strength. His energy was heavy, and I felt like I was going to burst into tears.

"Zachary, it looks like you don't feel well. What is going on?" He didn't even look up at me.

"Zachary, come on; do you want to go outside together? Want to go get ice cream? How about a walk, and we'll walk until we find a dog to pet?" His neck stayed leaning over, and he slowly turned his right eye up to gaze at me. No smile.

I racked my brain to think of something that would help. I had an idea. I drove to the Incredible Edible store where they dip fruit into chocolate. I placed an order, did some errands, and then picked them up and went back to the group home where Zachary lived. As I opened up the box, I showed them to Zachary and took a photo. I wondered if I could lure

Zachary into feeling better with a special treat. I marched into the kitchen to puree the chocolate covered strawberries, scooped up Zachary's chin, and opened his mouth. He barely swallowed ¼ teaspoon of dessert and dropped his head again. Zachary did the nano-second fake smile to let me know that he was trying hard to be who I wanted him to be. This was his way of saying, "I'm here, and I see you, and this is all I've got."

The next day, I talked with the house manager, and we agreed to take him to the doctor. There were not any signs to treat or diagnose, though she recommended we go get some blood work done. She would give us a call when the results came back. I went back to work. Zachary went to get some blood drawn and then back to his group home to sleep.

On October 4 at 3:35PM, the doctor called my cell phone and asked where I was. She said that she got the results and Zachary's sodium was high; he needed to go back to the children's hospital in Denver, which was an hour and a half away.

I did my quick assessment of the situation. In my mind, sodium was an innocent thing like table salt. So, I thanked her for the follow-up phone call. She asked if I could leave work to take him to the hospital. Again, I quickly assessed the situation and brainstormed some options. I told her that I could leave work, though my preference was to finish what I was doing, grab the quick date night Mike and I had scheduled for 7:30PM, and then I could swing by to pick up Zachary and pop in the hospital.

She was kind and clear.

"Zachary needs to go the hospital now. You can take him, or I will call an ambulance to take him to Denver."

I am pretty quick to pick up on verbal cues, and it was becoming clear that she thought this innocent table salt was a bigger issue than I did. By this time in my life, I learned to go along with experts who knew more than I, even if I felt no sense of urgency myself. She said she would call the ER immediately, so that he could get admitted.

It wasn't until Zachary was discharged 13 days later that I understood the severity of what had happened. I learned more about the miracle of the brain. I learned about the miracle of water. In the end, Zachary had become severely dehydrated. He was more interested in flirting with people who offered him a drink than actually drinking, and it could have cost him his life. Zachary, like most of us, yearned to connect in the most ordinary ways—to the point that having a moment with someone and no other agenda fed his soul. He would choose to stare into someone's eyes, smile, and hold that moment, rather than get distracted by tasks like eating, bathing, diaper changing, or drinking.

The brain can compensate for a super-high sodium level, though at some point it becomes really dangerous. If the body's sodium level is too high, and then the body gets a big swig of water to rehydrate, the brain cells go from being shriveled up to swelling up quickly and can put the body into an irreversible paralysis. If he had been given water without electrolytes too quickly, he could have become fully paralyzed for life.

Thank God for physicians who can create a holding environment for patients and families like us. Throughout this entire process, the teams of doctors were intimately focused on Zachary's well-being and gave me information one step at a time so that I could be with him every step of the way, and not be overwhelmed by the situation. They did what they are trained to do and kept meeting us where we were.

Zachary was in the hospital for fourteen days and discharged on October 17, 2013.

Mike had spent a lot of time with Zachary over the years. He had picked him up on Thursday nights to watch football and baseball together at the local sports bars. He has taken Zachary to Hooters for his birthday and invested a lot of one-on-one guy time with him. Mike has known Zachary well. He has been of Zachary's biggest champions.

So, I wasn't surprised when Mike asked if we could schedule some time to talk about something related to Zachary. I said sure, and then suggested we just talk right away. Mike agreed. We sat in the living room facing each other. I could tell Mike was hesitant and couldn't imagine why. Finally, he spoke.

"Sandy, I have noticed the frequency and severity of Zachary's hospitalizations are increasing. His hospitalizations started out every two years, then increased to every year, and now they are just four months apart. Have you noticed that?"

I hesitated and searched for the right word, "Nope."

"I wondered if we could talk about how we want to celebrate Zach's life."

Silence.

"I wanted us to begin to talk about how we might want to bring closure to Zach's life. We may need to start thinking about how to move on in our life without Zach."

I searched for something else to say, though I had already cut off and couldn't believe this is what Mike wanted to talk about. I couldn't deny what Mike was saying, though my mind was focused on the upcoming races Zachary was scheduled to race and his yoga classes he giggled through. I was busy coordinating logistics and relationships, and I didn't see any point in discussing the end-of-life topic any further. In fact, Zachary had completed 45 races, including 20 triathlons, and squealed on the zip line at summer camp. He was working out regularly, had a circle of great friends and was living a radically fulfilling life. I abruptly told Mike I would think about it, though I needed to go to the grocery store.

Three months later, January 27 2014, Zachary had extreme projectile vomiting of blood. It was worse than watching a horror movie. I think part of the awfulness was that he vomited repeatedly, and I couldn't tell when it was going to stop. As I stood in the local ER, beside the house manager from his group home, the nurses, technicians, and physicians were quietly working together to diagnose Zachary's new medical problem and replace blood-soaked linens with clean sheets. My eyes darted, paused, and then shifted from Zachary to the blood covering him, to the quiet healthcare team moving between the curtains that separated us from other ER patients. I hunched over to be shorter so I could stay close to Zachary. I insisted the ER team call the Fort Collins Youth Clinic to let the pediatrician on call know something terrible was happening. This was the exact opposite of the high-sodium incident just a few months before, where Zachary was silent and withdrawn, and his body looked normal on the outside. I was witnessing a violent eruption of blood hurtling out of his mouth.

Thankfully Dr. John Guenther, Zachary's pediatric physician from the Fort Collins Youth Clinic, was on call. He quickly assessed the situation and immediately admitted us to the ICU upstairs. We were transferred from the ER to Room 10 on the 3rd floor at 3:00AM.

Dr. Guenther sat beside us and talked until 5:00AM. Zachary fell asleep smiling at me. The doctor explained that Zachary may die of massive internal bleeding, perhaps sometime soon. I told him that I could not hear him. He suggested that Mike, Taylor, and I meet with him to talk about end-of-life issues. I cried. Then I stopped. I scooted closer to Zachary and asked Dr. Guenther to stay and talk to me. I asked him how it will look to be with someone who bleeds to death and what it will be like for Zachary. He sat beside us in the dark of the night and gently described how it could be peaceful for Zachary, like falling asleep. He said we would not be alone and introduced the role of people from hospice.

I do not have any idea what timeline we had to be together. Though I didn't like that feeling, I didn't want to know, either. As I sat in the dark with Zachary, a part of me was wilting, and a part of me was screaming. The only thing I felt thankful for was that Zachary was not in pain.

Before sunrise, Mike fed all the horses, dogs, and cats, and called Taylor in Boulder. Mike asked Taylor to drive to Fort Collins so we could meet as a family to talk about end-of-life issues for Zachary. Dr. Julie Brockway was the incoming pediatrician on call. When she walked in the room, she just sat beside me in silence. I whispered, "Mike tried to talk to me about this happening and I couldn't hear him. I still can't. This is too hard." By dawn, Mike, Taylor, Dr. Brockway and I sat beside Zachary's bed to begin the discussion Dr. John Guenther had suggested. Mike said I should go home to rest, while he and Taylor sat with Zachary. I had been up for 24 hours. He told me we were entering uncharted territory again, and we needed to take care of each other. He asked me to go home and sleep, and then go to my scheduled piano lesson. I was too sad to argue.

I went home and tried to write Zachary's memorial service. I was cut off from my emotions and exhausted with grief. I wrote a mechanical-sounding memorial service and collapsed into a deep sleep for three hours. When I woke up, I called Mike. He told me about a bright-eyed gastroenterologist physician for adults who'd come to see Zachary. The doctor said Zachary had esophageal varices and that he had success with a 'rubber-band' process to treat the varices. The pediatrician team had not heard of this procedure, though it was used in adults with these symptoms. As far as we knew, it would be a temporary solution, though we would know more after the procedure. I wanted to jump in my car to go to the hospital, but Mike asked me to go to my piano lesson first.

Mike knew that one of my happy places was taking piano lessons from Mark Sloniker. I had confessed to him that I didn't think they were really piano lessons; they were some kind of bliss appointments. I walked away from my piano lessons with my heart pounding with joy and my entire being lifted up and soaring through the next day.

At this piano lesson, instead of feeling joy, I sat in front of the keyboard and cried. I asked Mark questions of grief and loss. He listened and we played quiet music together.

That evening Zachary went in and out of surgery and, by the next morning, was eating small bites of pancakes with syrup, using the remote control to get some music in the room, and smiling from his head to his heart. We had a family meeting scheduled with hospice on Thursday and the Boulder triathlon three days later on Sunday. Someone forgot to send Zachary the memo that his body was struggling. He just smiled and was willing and able to connect with anyone else who could also get present and live one moment at a time.

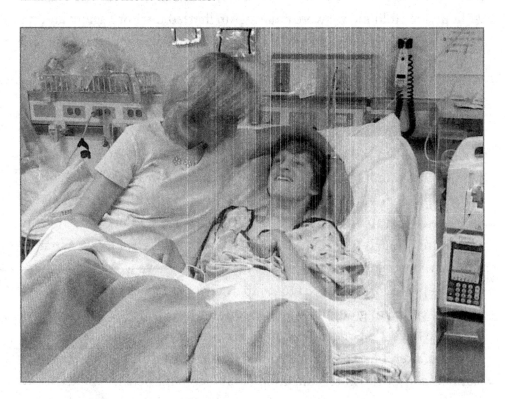

Before discharge, I sat close to Zachary. I had tears of hope and joy dripping from my cheeks. "Does Zachary still need to go to hospice?" I asked his doctor.

Our pediatrician just smiled. "No, I'll cancel the Hospice meeting. Zachary needs to do what he loves to do. Go enjoy the Boulder triathlon, and then we'll talk next week about a follow-up procedure with the gastroenterologist."

Zachary and Dennis completed the Boulder Sunrise Triathlon just like they had so many times before.

CHAPTER 15

CALM AFTER THE STORM

In the autumn of 2014 we were informed that all group homes in northern Colorado were going to close. The agency was supporting a national vision to provide more person-centered care, and group homes did not provide this. I never expected this news, so I said something polite and then wrapped up the phone call quickly. I didn't want to talk about it.

During that following week, many of the past conversations about Zachary's medical complexities haunted me. I remembered how we were told at the time of discharge from various hospital visits that Zachary may need to move to a traditional nursing home. His care was increasingly beyond the scope of the staff at the group home, so I couldn't imagine another setting that could support Zachary. In fact, I remembered an annual meeting where one of the agency directors commented upon how Zachary ranked as one of the top 10 most medically complex residents they supported, yet he was also ranked as one of the top 10 most active in the community.

Mike and I talked. He suggested we consider bringing Zachary home. His perspective was logical and heartfelt; we had built our house to be universally accessible. He said it was the right thing to do. I said no. The dialogue started and stopped in two sentences. Mike walked away upset, discouraged that I'd cut off from him and found no value in his idea. I felt deep grief at making this choice and anger that the group homes were closing, like I was being crucified on a rock wall with no escape route.

When I feel like there are no options, I silently blame everyone. In this case, I blamed the people who told me the news and any organization affiliated with them. I was convinced that this challenge was going to be the one to take me down. I was scared I would suffocate. I knew what it felt like to not be able to breathe, and I was overwhelmed with a sense of not getting enough "oxygen" in my life if I tried to balance raising Zachary at home and work full time, especially since Mike and I were now in our 50s and 60s. How would Mike and I be able to take care of Zachary's daily needs, provide him with a meaningful life, and continue taking care of ourselves as aging parents?

In the midst of my internal temper tantrum, I climbed up onto the balcony of my life. I told myself to think about the situation through the lens of dreaming big. I told myself to be still and take one daily action. I started with no dreams. My daily meditations lasted less than a minute. I just closed my eyes, waited, and then told myself, "There. I did the stupid meditation." My daily walk was around the car before I got in it. That was all I had in me.

Then Karey, one of Zachary's providers, called and said that she had a vision of Zachary living with a host family—and she knew just the family. I explained that was very kind of her to think of us, but it would not work. Zachary's medical needs were very intense, and according to any data I reviewed, host-family turnover with a person like Zachary could vary from two to more families each year. Living with that rate of change sounded like chaos on a good day and full of fake relationships on a bad one. Granted, I was skeptical how anyone could do this if I, his own mother, didn't have the capacity for it.

Karey, a highly intuitive and compassionate soul, ignored me. She called Alexis, a woman who had worked at Crescent House as a manager in previous years and had a strong connection with Zachary. Together they talked about the possibilities. Alexis and her husband Bobby consider themselves blue-collar gypsies who believe strongly in working hard and giving everything else they have to love—love for Bobby's children, love for their families, and love for each other and their values. Alexis is a dreamer and is often labeled naïve, as she comes up with ideas of many possible, and even seemingly impossible, hopes for the things that she is passionate about. She is a natural-born caregiver and a third-generation family member who had worked with the developmentally disabled. Alexis was meant to play this role even before she was aware that it could be an option.

Alexis called me as I was sitting in Mike's office, and I listened. When it was my turn to speak, I repeated my perspective: his medical needs were too much for one family to manage. "Alexis, I appreciate that you love Zachary, and that means a lot to me. I also know that I would not be able to do this—and I am his mom. Why do you think you can?"

She listened; then she shared her visions of possibilities, and I could feel her sense of deep presence. She began speaking to me in a way that went straight to my heart. As I listened to her describing why it would work for her, her family, and Zachary, I felt something I hadn't felt before. I exhaled air I had been holding in for decades. My shoulders dropped; my heart slowed and softened. I stopped pacing the floor and slowly curled into the corner of our artificial leather sofa. "Sandy, I got goose bumps on my body when Karey called me," Alexis continued. "This is hard for me to say, but I wanted to have children and was not able to. Zachary and I have always had a strong connection. What if it's possible that you got to raise him his first 21 years, and now I could step in and support him during his adult years?"

I felt like that day we'd gone to Crested Butte and the ski instructors had bigger plans for Zachary than I did. The instructors, like Alexis, had an awareness of something that was possible that I could not see and a passion and personal experience that were true and genuine.

We scheduled a time for Alexis and her husband to come to our home to talk with Mike and me. Zachary didn't come because I wanted the four of us to talk openly and candidly. Taylor was at school in Boulder, and we would keep him informed of the situation.

The day came, and the four of us sat on the porch with glasses of water and no agenda. Mike started with a question for Bobby, a tall, lean man with tattoos and a pierced lip. "Bobby, when I met Sandy and decided to spend my life with her, I knew that part of the package included Zachary and Taylor. You and Alexis are married, and you have your own blended family. Why would you do this?"

Bobby was thoughtful. "When Alexis and I got married, she knew Zachary and talked about him. Then the job of managing the administrative part of the position became cumbersome, so we moved to Denver. I lost a part of my wife, and ever since she has been thinking about this new role of being a host family, she is glowing, and I feel like I am getting her back."

We talked about the stresses of blended families, navigating sleepless nights, and medical appointments. We talked about divorce, marriage, family, and each of our values. We slowly began to design our relationship by honestly talking about hopes, dreams, fears, and concerns. By the end of the week, we had made a plan and started down the path of imagining what could be possible with Alexis and Bobby as Zachary's host family. Unlike other host families, where the adult with the disability moved into a family's home, Alexis and Bobby would move into Zachary's new home.

After that conversation I began to feel something soften inside of me. I stopped judging the agency for closing the group home. I started to hear their vision of assisting residents to live in more person-centered environments. I stopped telling myself that group homes were the only option for Zachary and started to notice how sad and increasingly disengaged Zachary had actually become living in the group home. I had been ignoring the impact of Zachary's roommates who'd disappeared. Because of HIPAA and confidentiality issues, I pretended like I didn't notice when roommates passed away during the night, or went to the hospital and didn't come back. During the time Zachary lived at Mosaic, I had felt so scared that I couldn't take care of Zachary at home that I ignored the depressing side of living there. Feeling I had limited choices, I told myself everything was just fine.

Eventually, a series of conversations began to unfold. Zachary, Mike, Taylor, and I started to dream big. We began daily phone calls with Alexis and her husband, who were living in Denver. We met with agencies involved in Zachary's current and future care. Our family started to see the picture about the possibilities for Zachary. We had been renting the condominium where I had lived with the boys as a single mom. The renter's agreement ended December 31st. We contacted the renter and told her we would be renovating it for Zachary to move into beginning January 1st.

Together we focused on Zachary and his ideal life, on how to design his room at 1808 Centennial Road to meet his needs and how to re-establish a sense of well-being that would be meaningful to him. Essentially, we brainstormed a list of 25 wishes for the next chapter in his life. Some of them were:

1. We wish he had a deep bathtub to soak in each night; Zachary loves swimming.

2. We wish he could live with a puppy; Zachary loves animals.

3. We wish he could attend yoga 2x/week; Zachary smiles in environments with less talking, more breathing.

4. We wish he could swim every week; Zachary's muscle tone relaxes after swimming.

5. We wish he could have more one-on-one connections, not just when someone is feeding or dressing him.

6. We wish he could live walking distance to a pool: go there often in summer.

7. We wish he could live walking distance to a grocery store: walk there often.

8. We wish he lived in a neighborhood where people knew him.

9. We wish friends and family could hang out at his home in a healing and non-medical environment.

10. We wish he could access more culture; people of different languages; international connections.

11. We wish he could participate in more daily chores, rather than sitting helplessly.

12. We wish he could explore one-on-one intimacy in ways that are personally meaningful to him.

13. We wish he could participate in a weekly meditation or worship service among a community.

14. We wish he could be more engaged in local community volunteering/ service.

15. We wish he could be among people so that he grows his hobbies, rather than doing the same things he'd been doing 15 years ago.

Essentially, we looked at Zachary's Life Wheel and opened up the floodgates. As we began to dream big about Zachary's future, Alexis ran with it. As she brought more of herself to the conversation of possibilities, we saw a bigger world for Zachary.

Zachary has begun the next chapter of his life, and it is far beyond any dream I originally had. Zachary is no longer living my dream; he is finding his own way. He is a young man who brings optimism and positive

energy to each day. In doing so, he evokes some mysterious kind of reci-
procity with others. Just like Mike and I practice our mantra of "You, me,
us" for our relationship to thrive, Zachary has non-verbally launched his
own version of how to engage in relationships. He seems to be inviting
others to a relationship that begins with a knowing that "As I bring all
of me, and you bring all of you, we will open up a new frontier together."

My outside world seemed to be smooth and in good order. Zachary
and his host family had all the makings of an ideal life. Taylor was about
to graduate from college. Mike and I were spending more time outdoors,
spending more time together as a couple, and navigating all the system
changes to support Zachary to live in his own condo. Yet something still
felt disconnected inside of me.

I went to visit the counselor I had seen in 2005 to do EMDR work.
She recommended I reflect deeply on how I had supported my kids. She
asked me to notice how I felt about myself in raising the boys. She was
not interested in my accomplishments or what I had done as their mom.
Rather, she was interested in how I felt. The assignment sounded easy
enough, though my initial responses felt fake and from my head.

On a business trip to St. Louis, Laurie asked me what was on my mind.
Laurie Cure was the CEO of a consulting company, Innovative Connections.
I worked as an executive & physician coach for IC during the early mornings and on my days off from my corporate job. There we sat at a trendy
360 restaurant overlooking the arch, and I told her about my ridiculous
assignment. Actually, my ridiculous inability to do the assignment.

Logically I could tell myself that I had done my best in raising the
boys, though in my heart, I felt as if each of the boys had scars invisible

to others. I could see and feel the wounds that had left their marks. I was fully aware of how I had spent most of my energy pulling them forward into a safe place in the future while stomping out any reminders of how they had been discounted and marginalized during the years they lived in New Hampshire. As we sipped cocktails, I began to find my voice for the first time to acknowledge my role in their lives. It didn't make any sense that this took so long for me to feel. Though I knew what to take a stand for, and I had a knowing of where to put my attention since the time of their births, the actual ability to rest into knowing who I was as a mom took a long time.

That night in the restaurant, above the city lights, I could feel things for the first time, a sense of knowing that:

1. I had a meaningful relationship with my kids.

2. I met them where they are so they could become who they are.

3. I allowed for Zachary and Taylor to find their authentic selves at an early age.

4. Early in their lives, I created a bubble and shield so they could each expand into their sense of self within the bubble.

5. I allowed the world to see Zachary and Taylor in a way that might not have happened otherwise.

Laurie sat with me and listened. She heard me. She heard all of me. I often forget how healing it is to feel heard and to be seen, how intimate life is when I share a point of vulnerability when I would rather talk about someone else.

On the day of Taylor's graduation, May 9, 2015, it was pouring rain. Mike and I drove to the University of Colorado stadium. I did not ask Taylor if his dad was coming. I did not want to induce a single sentence of heartache—just celebrate Taylor's incredible academic achievements. We arrived an hour early. Mike had graduated from CU forty years before and told me stories about what it was like for him to be a chemical engineer ready to move to Texas and work for Dow Chemical. The music started, and my eyes swelled with tears; I felt a total moment of peace wash over me, and all of my hidden agendas disappeared. I felt an absence of working or forcing something to happen ahead of its time. After the ceremony, we took pictures inside the dry stadium as people bumped into each other and hugged families of roommates they met for the first time. I took a risk and asked Taylor if his dad had come to watch him graduate, and he said yes. Jonathan had sat directly across from us on the opposite side of the stadium.

Taylor was graduating as a Mechanical Engineer and had accepted an amazing job offer to be a marine engineer. He would be based in Boulder and travel internationally to connect with clients and create real-time solutions for people. The position he accepted was almost exactly what he gave voice to on the porch in Estes Park at the Flow conference by Mihaly Csikszentmihalyi. I remember how he sat in one place on the porch describing the heaviness of what he didn't want to do and then abruptly got up, walked to another place, explored another perspective of the same situation, and by early evening was describing his personal ambitions and professional aspirations. He was working hard and creating his future to work authentically and serve wholeheartedly. I felt a sense of deep awe for who Taylor was becoming.

During Taylor's freshman year at CU, he met Emily in a Calculus class. Emily looked like she walked right off the cover of an REI catalog or Outside magazine. She was 6' tall and equally skilled in canoeing 45 miles of wilderness, leading a youth group of junior high girls, or solving complex problems. She was an accomplished artist, emerging entrepreneur and graduating as an aerospace engineer. Taylor and Emily spent time with friends during their college years studying, hiking, studying, scuba diving, studying, bicycling and watching the stars. They were true to themselves, each other and on a journey of exploring their faith and future together. Mike, my mom, dad, sisters, brother-in-law and I got to watch them graduate together. It was a total moment.

We decided not to bring Zachary to the CU graduation ceremony, though he would be at Taylor's graduation party/house concert that evening. On the walk back to Taylor's house after the ceremony, he and I spontaneously walked into a local liquor store on his corner. We bought a mini bottle of champagne and popped the cork outside in the early summer drizzle. I asked Taylor what he was feeling. He offered me a sip of the champagne first. I was so excited I tipped the bottom of the bottle up towards the sky for a big, graceless sip. It felt like it was about to squirt right out my nose. I pretended like I was a lady and didn't notice what had just happened, then I handed him the bottle. He glanced at me with a twinkle in his eye, took a sip, then put both arms in the air above his 6'7" body and declared with a beaming smile "I feel like the comeback of the century! Woot! Woot!" Taylor draped his heavy arm, like the wing of a California Condor, across my shoulder. "Mom, the single greatest present I have ever been given, um other than the gift of life was learning TM. Thank you for the best gift ever, and thank you for believing in me." We squeezed each other as we strolled along in the drizzle. Taylor was beaming and said, "I love you so much."

Taylor had taken risks, fallen, and gotten up again. He had the courage to make mistakes and ask for forgiveness. He allowed life to touch him, impact him, and through the rubble was finding his voice. He was cultivating his own awareness of his values, his hopes and dreams. He had worked hard to build a bridge from his heart to the world he was about to enter.

That night, it rained so hard in Bellvue that one of the two roads to our home was closed due to flooding. Guests from out of town had to turn around and drive back into town for cell coverage and then call to ask how else to get there. The rain turned to snow as people parked their cars in the pasture and walked in between the puddles in the red clay driveway. Eventually, our home filled with friends, families, and roommates. A musician with a dreamy voice sang "Better Together" and "Banana Pancakes" as Emily's sister and grandmother walked over to meet Zachary. Michelle, our former childcare provider, was a mom tonight and introduced her two young daughters to Zachary. Animated and giggling, he flirted with everyone who plopped down next to him. Bobby filled a plate with Texas BBQ, homemade sweet potato salad, and chocolate cake with raspberry sauce for Alexis and Zachary to eat.

Taylor allowed me to grab the microphone and speak from my heart. As I glanced across the room, words spilled out of me, full of humor, gratitude, and appreciation for each family, neighbor or friend who'd come to celebrate Taylor.

The day after the party, Taylor, Emily, and another couple celebrated by taking a three-week tour of the national parks across the west. Coincidentally, they followed a similar path of the trip Taylor and I had taken back when he was just eight years old. This trip also mirrored a motorcycle trip my dad and I had taken when I attended the University of Iowa in 1987: Rocky Mountain National Park, Bryce Canyon, Zion Canyon, Sequoia National Park, oh yeah—and Las Vegas. Taylor and Emily also visited Spirit Lake and then launched their new lives and their new careers in Boulder.

Throughout the years, I have established stronger meditation, walking, and yoga practices. I've become more present to what has unfolded in my life. I've made different choices about what to take a stand for and what to let go of.

Having spent much of my life as a people pleaser, I did not have much experience with anger. But I've become increasingly aware of feelings of hurt and anger. I have learned to pay attention to these feelings and walk right into them. Rather than cutting off, I practiced the tips my counselor recommended to me as healthy ways to express these emotions. I've learned how to leverage new breathing techniques in times of stress, address conflict in new ways, and practice stronger boundaries.

During my coach training, I learned the skill of reframing difficult life experiences, though I would unconsciously leave myself out of the equation. I have now learned to put myself back into the equation when reframing situations. It did not come naturally, and my default is still to accommodate what others need. This will be a lifelong workout for me.

We can apply a coaching mindset to support ourselves, families, systems, and world to be a better place. In order to do this, I personally needed to unpack my fears of living a broken life with a depressing future and embrace the mystery of the unknown. Little did I know that what started out as a baby's diagnosis of multiple complex disabilities would actively reframe my own understanding of a world of possibilities.

A lifetime journey of discovery, chaos, hopelessness, hopefulness, and curiosity has quieted my fears, assumptions, and beliefs. I now feel increased moments of awe as my family and I explore ways to connect to a future of possibilities that support us to be our best selves so that we can live, love, and lead more fully. It has been a gift to share my journey.

Jared Seger Photos, Gilbert AZ

ACKNOWLEDGMENTS

The purpose of the book emerged as I found myself writing about how we can leverage difficult experiences to live meaningful lives.

The reason I wrote this book is to try to make sense of my life since graduating from college. I was surprised to find that writing this book was an actual microcosm of my actual life. In raising Zachary and Taylor, I can now tell that I was able to leverage my creativity, discipline, and desire to expose my inner awareness. I see more vividly how I was able to use these qualities in my life to create a meaningful life and that others can, too!

I give thanks to the many remarkable people who impacted my life and our family's life in the extremely ordinary ways. Thank you to the friends we have known before the boys were born. Thank you to the friends and providers we have spent time with since Zachary's birth. A special thanks to the people who have seen each of us and allowed us to see you. Thank you for seeing us as whole and being in the conversation of growing ourselves beside each other. I feel overwhelmed with grace to have friends, family, colleagues, acquaintances, and providers who have paused so that we can be real with each other, if only for a moment. A heartfelt thank-you to my editor Alexia for helping me organize this story.

The book is a gift to myself, my family, and others to have deeply meaningful lives.

People influenced me in many ways. Some of the thought leaders who encouraged me to step into the future and consider new ways to living a meaningful life include the following.

A READING LIST
TO NAVIGATE YOUR FUTURE

Social Inventors & Advocates for inclusion

- **Snow, Judith.** *What's Really Worth Doing & How To Do It.* The book details the personal story of helping Judith Snow move out of an institution and into the community. The message is powerful and simple: None of us can deal with a crisis alone.

- **Norman Kunc.** *The Broad Reach Center for Training, Counseling & Mediation on Disability Issues.* As counselors & presenters, Norman is interested in exploring the alternative narratives that enable people with disabilities to discover the unique contribution they make in our society.

Attorneys

- **Joseph Jaworksi.** *Synchronicity: The Inner Path of Leadership.* Jaworski was elected as a fellow of The American College of Trial Lawyers, an honor awarded to the top 1% of American litigators. In 1980, Joseph founded the American Leadership Forum, a non-governmental organization dedicated to strengthening collaborative civic leadership in the United States. He devoted much of his life to exploring the deeper dimensions of transformational leadership. As founder and chairman of both Generon International and the Global Leadership Initiative, Joseph collaborates with leaders who are committed to developing the capacities for innovation and transformation that results in fundamental change both in themselves and in their organizations.

The book presents his personal philosophy of life. It illustrates that leadership is about the release of human possibilities, about enabling others to break free of limits created organizationally or self-imposed.

Scientists & Researchers

- **Peter Senge.** *Working with Presence: A Leading with Emotional Intelligence Conversation with Peter Senge Audio.* The ideas expressed in Emotional Intelligence ten years ago have taken on a life of their own. They spurred a movement, with enthusiastic adherents in the business world, in medicine and healthcare, at home in the field of education and the world at large.

- **Candice Pert.** *Molecules of Emotion: The Science Behind Mind-Body Medicine.* Why do we feel the way we feel? How do our thoughts and emotions affect our health? Are our bodies and minds distinct from each other, or do they function together as parts of an interconnected system?

- **Dr. Joan King.** *A Life on Purpose: Wisdom at Work.* The book examines not just new business models, but also new ways of perceiving business. Dr. Joan King simplifies the complexities of business by guiding the reader through an understanding of how the body simplifies complex systems to run efficiently, cooperatively, and harmoniously.

- **Dr. Joan Borysenko.** *A Woman's Journey to God: Finding the Feminine Path.* I flipped through pages of this book as a single mom grabbing facts, stories and inspiration to strengthen my faith.

Sociologists & Psychologists

- **Mihaly Csikszentmihalyi.** *New resource: www.pursuit-of-happiness. org. Mihaly's most recent research shows how "the best moments usually* *occur if a person's body or mind is stretched to its limits in a voluntary effort to accomplish something difficult and worthwhile." (1990, pg. 3)*

- **Parker Palmer.** *Best resource: www.couragerenewal.org. The Center for Courage & Renewal provides a wide range of resources, including books, journals, and blogs. I just discovered him after Zachary moved out of our home and into his own place.*

Poets

- **David Whyte.** *The Three Marriages: Reimagining Work, Self and Relationship.* The book shares from his own struggles and exploring the lives of some of the world's great writers & artists to show the ways our core commitments are connected. We discover how to bring our roles together in one fulfilled life. Also audio series: *What to Remember When Waking: The Disciplines of an Everyday Life.*

- **Mary Oliver.** *Best resource: www.onbeing.org Mary Oliver.* I gained a deeper understanding of some of my own feelings and life experiences listening to Krista Tippett's interview with Mary Oliver. Their conversation opened up new spaces in my heart as I walked along the trails near our home.

Economics, Business & Research

- **Otto Scharmer.** *Theory U: Leading from the Future as It Emerges. The Social Technology of Presencing.* Theory U proposes that the quality of the results we create in our lives and any kind of social system is the result of the quality of awareness, attention, or consciousness that we operate from. He describes the impact of what can happen when we shift the inner place from which we operate.

- **Marcus Buckingham.** *First Break All the Rules & Now, Discover your Strengths.* I used these books to guide the conversations I had with

CNAs and childcare providers when the boys were little. I was inspired by the research demonstrating how we grow more by focusing on our strengths. His books outline practical steps to apply this in our own lives and the teams we work with.

- **Jim Collins.** *Great by Choice.* Jim is a student and teacher of leadership and has personally touched our lives. Jim's Chief Operating Officer, Dave Sheanin, has partnered with Zachary in triathlons and is an amazing champion of possibilities. Jim's books focus on successful habits of visionary companies and the uncertainty, chaos, and luck of others. *Great by Choice* outlines why some companies thrive and others don't. I find his principles extremely relevant to any type of systems change.

Musicians

- **Mark Sloniker.** *CD recordings: www.marksloniker.com.* My favorites are True Nature and Paths of Heart. Mark is my piano teacher, even though I only take lessons randomly as my schedule allows and my spirit has the courage to show up. Mark reminds me I don't need to practice like the gremlin in my head keeps telling me—rather explore and play from a gentler place.

- **Loreen McKennitt.** *DVD concert to watch: Nights from the Alhambra.* This is an incredibly soulful live album and DVD from 2006 recorded in Spain. The music combines Celtic/folk/world beat. The mood ranges from dreamy and reflective to intense. I watched it over and over; then I had the chance to watch her and the 12-piece band play at Lyon's Folk Festival just a few miles away.

Artists

- **Carrie Fell.** *Fine Art Serigraphs*: I was so attracted to Carrie's dramatic use of tropical color with western wildlife. Her work helped me to connect to the western landscape and horses, which originally looked a bit brown, sterile and boring to me.

- **Julia Cameron.** *The Right to Write.* Julia's work introduced me to the concept of an Artist Date. She promoted the idea of a once-weekly, festive, solo expedition to explore something that interests you. Later, I discovered her book *The Right to Write* and felt completely liberated to write 1,000 words every morning, which turned into this book.

Priest-Pastor-Rabbi

- **Ilia Delio.** *Making All Things New: Catholicity, Cosmology, Consciousness.* Ilia is a Franciscan Sister of Washington, DC and American theologian who introduces a new paradigm for being. She demonstrates the conscious awareness of how everything—sun and stars, maple trees and muddy rivers, and all organisms from the single-celled to homo sapiens—forms one thing. She describes the power to reconnect all the dimensions of life: spirituality, religion, the new sciences, culture and society.

- **Matthew Fox.** *The Reinvention of Work: New Vison of Livelihood for Our Time.* Fox has been considered a radical priest, showing visions of a world where our personal and professional lives are celebrated in harmony—a world where the self is not sacrificed for a job but is sanctified by authentic "soul work."

- **Nadia-Bolz Weber.** *Pastrix: The Cranky, Beautiful Faith of a Sinner & Saint.* I was completely surprised to discover a female religious figure speak so candidly and chock full of raw humor about faith in the most unexpected, yet ordinary ways.

- **Rabbi Rami Shapiro.** *Perennial Wisdom for the Spiritually Independent.* Rabi Shapiro is a self-proclaimed *luftmensch,* someone who lives in the rarified atmosphere of ideas. To him, religions are like languages; no language is true or false; all languages are of human origin. Judaism is his mother tongue, yet in matters of the spirit he strives to be multi-lingual. In the end, however, he claims the deepest language of the soul is silence.

- **Father Thomas Keating.** *The Human Condition.* One of the founders of the Centering Prayer movement, Thomas Keating offers a reflection on contemplative prayer, the human search for happiness and our need to explore the inner world.

- **Thomas Merton & Henri Nouwen.** *Becoming Who You Are: Insights on the True Self from Thomas Merton and other Saints.* Thomas Merton worked in corporate finance for six years and then studied to become a Jesuit priest. Henri Nouwen's vision of spirituality was broad and inclusive, and his compassion embraced all of humankind. I listened to people talk about both their writings, which were always so alive with meaning, inspiration and liberating.

- **Father Richard Rohr.** *Everything Belongs.* In this guide to prayer, Richard Rohr encourages readers to think afresh, forget old habits, and accept what comes. Rohr is the internationally acclaimed author of *Discovering the Enneagram.*

Physicians

- **Francine Gailour, MD.** *CEO of Physician Coaches Institute.* Gailour is a physician, pioneer, and founder of the PCI. Her mission is to catalyze change and innovation in healthcare. She trained me and other coaches to expertly coach physicians and healthcare teams. I now serve on the PCI Advisory Board, where we serve as the creative center for healthcare-coaching best practices and guide the future vision of physician leadership.

- **Ronald Heifetz, MD.** *Leadership Without Easy Answers.* This book changed the way I understood leadership and my role as a mom, leader, speaker, and coach. Heifetz offers a practical approach to leadership for us when we are leading as well as when others are leading us. Drawing on a dozen years of research, Heifetz presents clear, concrete prescriptions for any of us; as patients, physicians, executives, families, or volunteers.

- **Rachel Remen, MD.** *Kitchen Table Wisdom and Grandfather's Blessings.* I read these books to care providers before they started a shift, to healthcare leaders during hospital New Employee Orientation, to friends and family in hospice. Remen, a physician, therapist, professor of medicine, and long-term survivor of chronic illness, is a down-home storyteller.

Mystics and Catholic Visionaries

- **Caroline Myss.** *CMED Online Institute.* I listened to Caroline's audio-cassettes when the boys were younger, though she now offers online courses. They offer transformational concepts, inspiring ideas, spiritual truths, and sacred mysteries that draw you into wondrous states of deep reflection about your life and power you have to redirect your life at any given moment.

- **Hildegard of Bingen.** I don't have a specific reference, though I was captured by stories of Bingen. As a woman in the 12th century, she used the term "visio" to describe experiences she had that she could not explain to others. I love how Hildegard explained that she saw all things in the light of God and experienced God through the five senses: sight, hearing, taste, smell, and touch. From what I understood, Hildegard was hesitant to share her visions. I often felt this way, too, as a mom.

- **Julian of Norwich.** I don't know much about Julian, either. I was attracted to the glimpses of how she was able to describe her visions of God with clarity and depth. Although she lived in a time of turmoil, her theology was optimistic and spoke of God's love in terms of joy and compassion.

- **Meister Eckhart.** I first learned the phrase "'no man can serve two masters" and thought about this through the lens of Eckhart, a Christian mystic. This simple phrase resonated with me especially as a mom and a leader navigating many complex systems. I liked to listen to people who described the way he could weave together metaphysics, spiritual psychology, and sermons.

Journalists and Writers

- **Maria Popova.** *BrainPickings.org, a blog.* Popova is known for her weekly blog featuring her writing on culture, books, eclectic subjects related to creativity, and the human experience. "If something interests me and is both timeless and timely, I write about it." This aligns with my sentiments in raising Zachary. If people offered resources or ideas to our family and it made sense for two or more of us, then it would interest me. In other words, I appreciate people who look for information and inspiration that is timeless, timely, and inclusive in intent.

- **Krista Tippett.** *On Being, radio show.* Tippett is an American journalist, author, and entrepreneur. I enjoy listening to her public radio Sunday afternoon show while I am walking. Krista uses a conversational approach to explore fresh and new ways to relate to each other.

Thought leaders in business, leadership, and change

- **Warren Bennis.** *On Becoming a Leader.* Bennis was a scholar, organizational consultant, and author, widely regarded as a pioneer of the contemporary field of leadership studies. His book introduced practical ways leaders could work in a less hierarchical, more democratic and adaptive way. I underlined something on most pages.

- **Ken Blanchard.** *All of his books along with his Situational Leadership Model.* Ken Blanchard is one of the most influential leadership experts in the world. His groundbreaking work in the fields of leadership and management includes a phenomenal vision for Blanchard coaching to democratize coaching. This means they are passionate about making coaching easy and affordable for corporate sponsors to provide to the people who want it and need it.

- **Marshall Goldsmith.** *What Got You Here Won't Get You There.* Goldsmith has been recognized as one of the top ten most influential business thinker in the worlds and the top-ranked executive coach at the 2013 Biennial Thinkers50 ceremony in London. This book describes the "transactional flaws" we as people have which lead to negative perceptions and can hold us back. This book is straightforward and loaded with jargon-free advice.

- **John Kotter.** *Leading Change.* This book is used by millions worldwide. I have used this book as a mother to guide systems changes impacting Zachary's life and as an executive/physician coach. Jonathan's now-legendary eight-step process for managing change with positive results has become the foundation of how I think about change for organizations, teams, or the systems we work with.

- **Jonathan C. Maxwell.** *21 Irrefutable Laws of Leadership.* Maxwell uses short stories to remind us of how leadership comes only from influence and can't be mandated. He is an internationally recognized leadership expert, speaker, coach, and author.

Leadership Consultant

- Innovative Connections Inc. *www.innovativeconnectionsinc.com* An incredible consulting company working with individuals and organizations to expand capacity to achieve stronger personal and organizational results. Contact us: 970-690-9700.

Education & Information Promoting Inclusion

- Specifically, in Colorado, I recommend the PEP conference found at *www.cde.state.co.us* It is a parent-focused conference. It is designed to promote partnerships that are essential in supporting and including children with disabilities and their families in schools and communities.

- *www.care.com* article "10 Helpful Special Needs Organizations" lists current organizations dedicated to supporting families of young children with disabilities to flourish. My experience is to reach out and explore the kinds of education, innovation, and connections that feel right to each of us as families.

- National Early Childhood Technical Assistance System: NEC*TAS provides technical assistance to assist and support states, Early Education Programs for Children with disabilities, implementation of Part H to expand and improve services to young children with special needs and their families.

- Early Childhood Technical Assistance Center: Improving Systems, Practices & Outcomes for Infants and Toddlers with disabilities (Part C of IDEA). *www.ectacenter.org*

Want to connect?

1. Visit our website *www.SandyScottLLC.com* to be part of the emerging future.

2. Join us on Facebook (Sandy Scott LLC) and LinkedIn sites.

3. Host a reading group. For tips to host a book-reading group, see our website.

4. Invite Sandy as a guest author of a community book group or conference presenter.

THE EXTENDED PHOTO STORY
A few photos that didn't quite make the book.

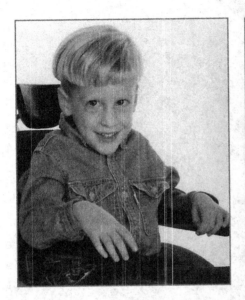

Jared Seger Photos, Gilbert AZ

The Best in Art and Life
Roger Rosenblatt

The best in art and life
comes from a center something urgent and powerful
an ideal or emotion
that insists
    on its being.

From that insistence
a shape emerges
    and creates its structure out of passion.

If you begin with a structure,
You have to make up the passion,
    and that's very hard to do.

Note: Prose text redone as a poem by Meg Wheatley.

CPSIA information can be obtained
at www.ICGtesting.com
Printed in the USA
FSOW04n0400111217
41980FS